Basic Witches

BASIC WITCHES

HOW TO SUMMON SUCCESS, BANISH DRAMA, AND RAISE HELL WITH YOUR COVEN

Jaya Saxena and Jess Zimmerman

Illustrated by Camille Chew

QUIRK BOOKS

PHILADELPHIA

Library of Congress Cataloging in Publication Number: 2016961079

ISBN: 978-1-59474-977-3

Printed in the United States of America

Typeset in Sabon, Meta, Brandon Grotesque, and Harbour

Designed by Andie Reid
Cover and interior illustrations by Camille Chew
Production management by John J. McGurk

Quirk Books
215 Church Street
Philadelphia, PA 19106
quirkbooks.com

10 9 8 7 6 5 4 3 2

CONTENTS

CHAPTER 3
Healing: The Power to Care for Yourself

CHAPTER 4
Summoning: The Power to Care for Others (and Have Them Care for You)

CHAPTER 5
Enchantment: The Power to Make Choices about Love and Sex

CHAPTER 6
Banishment: The Power to Avoid What Brings You Down

CHAPTER 7
Divination: The Power to Decide Your Destiny

SELF-INITIATION

Witches are everywhere these days. Fashion trends feature flowy black clothes and dark lipstick, magazines and websites run special witch-themed issues, and hipster covens are forming in Brooklyn.

What's so appealing about the witch? Partly, nostalgia. Women now in their twenties and thirties fondly remember growing up watching *The Craft* and *Sabrina the Teenage Witch*, reading Harry Potter, playing "light as a feather, stiff as a board" at slumber parties, or saving their allowance for a collectible light-up Hermione wand.

But the witch isn't kitsch. The modern witchy zeitgeist doesn't only glance backward into childhood; it looks forward to the future of powerful, defiant women. Witchcraft appeals to the weird, the outcast, and the unconventional; it has long been a spiritual practice belonging to those on society's fringes. And cultural images of witches, gleaned from history and movies and books and TV, resonate particularly with women who reject the strictures of expected female behavior, women who are trying to connect with something stronger and scarier.

In the original Old English, *witch* was a word that could apply to women and men alike. In fact, *wicca*—from which we get the word *witch*—can be directly translated as "male witch" or "sorcerer." But in the fifteenth century, witch-hunting guides like the *Malleus Maleficarum* argued that women were more inclined to witchcraft because they were inherently weak (physically, mentally, and spiritually) and susceptible to the devil's machinations.

This theory may sound ridiculous, but ideas like this have influenced notions of witchcraft—and, broadly, of women—for centuries. *Witch* quickly became a charge levied almost exclusively at women—particularly women who lived alone, outside the confines of the community. The witch was not beautiful, or she was (suspiciously) *too* beautiful; at any rate, she didn't look the way others thought she should. She refused men when they didn't appeal to her, pursued them when they did, and satisfied herself with that (wink, wink) "broomstick" she always "rode." She had cats instead of children. Other women came to her for care and comfort, but also turned on her when associating with her threatened their social standing.

The witch was intimidating, after all. Too strange. Too unruly. Too much.

But in mainstream modern U.S. culture, we've largely defanged the witch. Our cultural image is sometimes evil but sometimes silly, as if to suggest that the best way to counter things we don't understand is to laugh at them. Witches have green skin and warts and ride around on brooms yelling at children, and then they get houses dropped on them. Personally, our favorite pop-culture witches retain that old defiant, unruly nature; they're smart, strange, fearlessly ugly, sexy on their own terms. But for the most part, our culture no longer fears those traits in witches. Now, it mocks them.

Modern-day self-identified witches (and pagans and Wiccans, different groups that share some common beliefs) are trying to rescue the witch from haters and scoffers alike. They have resurrected old religions and traditions, and sometimes combined them, to create new communities. Witches of all stripes, from the religious to the spiritual to the secular, gather in covens or practice alone. Defying cultural stereotypes about witchcraft as dangerous or ridiculous, they find power in a goddess or nature or themselves.

This book isn't for them, though. They're all set. This book is for you.

Who Are You?

~~~

You're not necessarily a practicing witch. You might not believe in magic or mysticism or spirituality at all. But you're intrigued by the power, or the sisterhood, or the devil-may-literally-care attitude of the witches you've seen in pop culture and history. You don't think women should be considered frightening or ridiculous just because they don't toe the line.

You probably identify as a woman, but maybe you don't—maybe you're outside the gender binary, or maybe you're a man who's committed to justice for all. We are going to talk mainly about women in this book, because a lot of historical and cultural crap surrounding witches has been directed at women specifically. But we're also going to talk a lot about how societal notions of masculine and feminine—who can be which, and what they're worth—are total bullshit.

You might be into spiritualism and the occult. Maybe you don't believe tarot cards truly predict the future, but you still give yourself readings when you feel lost because the symbolism helps you tap into your hopes and fears. Maybe you've gotten together with friends to put a hex on your ex, not because you believed anything would happen but because it was fun and made you feel better. Maybe you've bought spells out of the backs of magazines just to see if they work, or maybe you dressed like the girls from *The Craft* because, hey, it's a good look.

Or maybe you're not into the myth and ritual at all. Maybe you're literal and pragmatic and you know for a fact that magic is not real. Maybe you don't think pretending otherwise is even helpful or fun. But you still appreciate the historical witch—the unruly woman, the woman who refuses to obey, the community healer with her cauldron of herbs—and recognize yourself in her. For you, a witch is any woman who understands she has power even when the world insists she doesn't.

Whether you wear all black and light candles for luck or you have no truck whatsoever with spells and witchy outfits, if you want to dismantle the cultural conditioning that trains women to be weak and small, you're in the right place. Welcome to our kind of witchcraft.

What We Mean by "Witchcraft"

~~~~~

Though it was once effectively a death sentence, the charge of *witchcraft* has never been supported with much evidence. We know women were *accused* of performing magic and consorting with the devil, but all we can truly know is that they pissed off someone in power, whether for performing an abortion or refusing to be Christian or saying "no" to a man. In this book, *witchcraft* doesn't mean occult or religious practices that historical witches may (or may not) have engaged in, nor does it mean the religious practice that is a sacred tradition for many people worldwide. We don't want to diminish that kind of witchcraft or lay claim to it. For our purposes, *witchcraft* means the kind of mundane pursuits that might once have resulted in accusation: enjoying sex, controlling reproductive health, hanging out with other women, not caring what men think, disagreeing, and just *knowing* stuff.

Our witchcraft is a cultural ethos. Our witchcraft is about rebellion—not for rebellion's sake, but with the purpose of living true to ourselves. That may mean embracing the traits you've been told make you weird, gross, insufficiently feminine. Many women are taught from an early age that any power we have, even power over ourselves, is considered dangerous, but witches revel in that danger. Ambition, assertiveness, nonconformity, high standards, the ability to say no, control over your own body: all witchcraft, by our definition. Our witchcraft also means practicing arts that may be devalued because they're *too* feminine: listening, supporting your friends, choosing clothes, applying makeup, crafts and cooking, taking care of people or animals, making and keeping friends, allowing yourself space. If you speak when you're told to be quiet, take pride when you're told to feel shame, love what and who you love whether or not others approve, you're practicing witchcraft.

Some of these abilities you're probably already in touch with. Others might be less familiar. You might feel ashamed for not being good at them naturally. ("I don't know anything about makeup. Why am I so bad at being a girl?") You might turn up your nose at them because you've been taught that they're unmasculine and therefore unserious. ("I don't care about feelings, I'm logical.") You might have deeply ingrained beliefs telling you that certain skills are off-limits. ("But if I speak up, people will think I'm such a bitch!")

But none of this power is beyond you. This witchcraft is your birthright—not just because you're a woman (if that's even how you identify) but because you're a person. Mainstream culture wants you to fit into a predefined role. Witchcraft enables you to find personal purpose, truth and intention. It allows you to discover the crafts, talents, and interests that make you *you*, without requiring that you recognize any one skill as superior or essential. You already have the potential to be a strong, self-actualized, powerful, ass-kicking witch. All you have to do is recognize your abilities, hone your skills, and channel them into making some magic.

What We Mean by "Magic"

This book cannot teach you to levitate, conjure wealth, or communicate with ghosts (though if you figure out how to do any of that, please call us!). What it *can* teach you are mantras, incantations, rituals, and other tiny spells that allow you to tap into your latent abilities and hidden power. Even if you know on some level that you can access and experience self-confidence, inner calm, and emotional acceptance, you might find doing so intimidating, embarrassing, or just plain difficult. The magic of this book will help you actualize those positive feelings. We'll talk about using magic to feel confident, to deal with your past, to envision your future, to break out of negative habits. You'll learn how to create an eternal bond by making hot chocolate, use crystals and talismans and tarot cards to harness power, and move through grief by making a friendship bracelet.

This magic might sound a little silly, but the theory behind it is simple logic: human brains are weird. (Everyone's! Not just yours.) Sometimes, the more you tell yourself to do something, the less you want to do it—even when it's something you really want to do, like supporting your friends in their successes, demanding the treatment you deserve at work, or generally valuing yourself. No matter our good intentions, we all make excuses to avoid doing what we know we *should* do. But rituals can redirect your focus, forcing your brain to subvert these excuses. Our version of modern magic is a means for navigating any mental obstacles that crop up—essentially, magic is a set of tricks to outwit yourself outwitting yourself. (We said brains were weird!) And it works. We know because we've made it happen ourselves.

This example sounds a little grim at first, but stick with us: back in 2001, soon after the terrorist attacks on the World Trade Center, letters containing live anthrax spores were delivered to a number of media outlets and congressional offices. Several people got sick, and five died. On the heels of 9/11, most Americans were already somewhere on the spectrum between traumatized and extremely tense, and for Jess, who lived in Washington, D.C., where some of the attacks took place, the anthrax sent that anxiety into overdrive. (How much overdrive? She broke out in stress hives, which of course she worried were cutaneous anthrax.) Jess knew that she was vanishingly unlikely to be an anthrax target, even accidentally—but she couldn't stop her brain from trudging over and over around the same irrational circular track.

But then her friend Kevin came through with a magical amulet. "What you need for anthrax," he said, "is wax. Public Enemy says very clearly in their song 'Bring the Noise' that 'wax is for Anthrax.' You should get some wax." Sure, this reasoning was patently ridiculous, but so was being worried. So Jess got a bit of wax, and knitted a little wax cozy for it, and carried it around with her, and instantly felt better. Why? Public Enemy aren't exactly wizards (except in the sense of being magically excellent musicians) and the wax was just wax—it didn't have any powers. But it kept Jess calm because its presence became a reminder to stop letting her brain chew itself to death with worry. And as such, it was an extremely effective magical talisman. The system works.

You may never experience anthrax anxiety, but you probably do have an equally specific problem that magic could help with. So we've grouped our magical suggestions into chapters on beauty, love, sex, friendship, and negative emotions. We encourage you to read through and experiment with all the spells in this book and to feel free to adapt them to suit your needs and comfort level. Do you feel silly speaking an incantation? That's fine; you can recite it in your head. Is one of the spell components too hard to source in your apartment at midnight on a Tuesday when you really need closure on your past relationship? That's fine—improvise! Think of our spells as starting points for recognizing all the astonishing ways in which you can communicate with your own brain and change the course of your thoughts and emotions. Of all the elements of a successful spell, your intention and desire for change are the only essential parts.

Meet Your Local Witches

We, Jess and Jaya, will guide you through your journey to witchy self-actualization, even though—well, sort of *because*—we're not witches in the traditional sense. We don't practice witchcraft as a religion, but we do see ourselves as continuing a long line of unruly women, refusing to let others define who we are or how we should be. Think of us as your Hagrids: we're here to bring the news that, by our definition, you're a witch already.

We're mostly like you: we've made bad love decisions, second-guessed ourselves, hated our bodies or faces sometimes, and tried to get through a whole day wearing uncomfortable shoes. We've worried about being pretty enough, successful enough, feminine enough, lovable enough, grounded enough. And eventually, after years of expending so much mental energy on these worries, we realized that a lot of this neurosis was coming from outside us. If we could cast off these ideas of what we should think and look like and be—if we could trick our brains into a better way of seeing with bespoke spells and rituals—we could get beyond those societal "shoulds" and into a safer, happier, more comfortable place.

But we also have a history of dabbling in witchcraft. Jaya cast her first spell when she was 12, to get her mom to let her go to Seth's bar mitzvah (it worked). She is a New Yorker who was born around Halloween, so black clothes and attraction to the creepy have always been part of her personal brand. She was raised without religion, but through a combination of influences from her Hindu grandmother, Quaker high school, and Jewish in-laws, she understands and appreciates the power of ritual. Jaya believes in intuition and that most spells are just a way to tap into it—a formalization of intent, a way to organize swirling thoughts by spending a moment alone with a candle or screaming in the woods. (Her tenth-great-grandparents may also have been hanged for witchcraft in Connecticut in the late 1600s, if Ancestry.com is to be believed.)

Jess is an aging goth and a comics reader, so she owns a lot of black clothes and skulls and has read a lot of those books about magick with a *k*—but she is also a lifelong atheist and doesn't believe in mysticism or the occult. She does believe in the human mind, though, and she's a big fan of using spells and rituals—though not necessarily those with candles and sage—to hack into and redirect mental habits. Also, and probably more importantly, she's a big mean feminist who wants to smash patriarchy, white supremacy, and whatever other systems of oppression look like they're cruisin' for a bruisin'. Jess is super into the witch as a woman who doesn't comply—either with demands that she be weak and malleable, or with gender norms that devalue some of her interests while making others off-limits.

We'll occasionally pop in to tell you stories about our personal relationships with magic and witchery, like the one about the wax. But our goal is to guide you through the process of finding, owning, and loving your own scary powers—whether that means building custom spells, finding new witchy role models, or just learning to embrace the parts of you that are too intimidating, too strange, too unruly, too much.

Let's start raising some hell.

OUR FAVORITE POP CULTURE WITCHES

THE DIFFICULTY IN FINDING witchspiration is separating fiction from truth. We know the names of historical witches like Marie Laveau and Tamsin Blight, but relatively little about their daily lives, and we definitely don't know whether they could indeed hex and curse, as myth now suggests. So if none of history's witches feel like the right role model, turn your attention to pop culture, which offers no shortage of badass, powerful witches to admire and emulate. Here are a few of our favorites and the specific skills they bring to the table.

WITCH: Hermione Granger
SKILL: Self-assuredness
One might be tempted to peg Hermione as a mere bookworm, but time and again she proves she contains multitudes. She's a fighter, a kind friend, and not above snagging an invite to the dance by flirting with the hot guy from out of town. Hermione is proof that if you believe in your own power, no one thing can define you. Only you get to define yourself.

WITCH: Tiffany Aching
SKILL: Intuition
The eponymous heroine of Terry Pratchett's young adult books learns to be a witch—and finds out that it's more about hard work and psychology than hocus-pocus. Tiffany can be impatient and a little conceited, but she's also loyal, sensible, extremely perceptive, and good at making cheese. She, and the witches who teach her, reminds us that sometimes

witchcraft is just a fancy word for keeping your house in order and caring for your own.

WITCH: Gillian Owens
SKILL: Rebelliousness
Gillian Owens is the wilder of the Owens sisters in *Practical Magic*. She's the one who'll get a tattoo on a dare, move across country just because she feels like it, and collect men like they're Pokémon. She's also a fiercely loyal and devoted sister, niece, and aunt. Sometimes her spontaneity gets the best of her, but, hey, sometimes the best way to get rid of a man is to hex his maple syrup.

WITCH: Sabrina the Teenage Witch
SKILL: Empathy
Sabrina is the type of witch many of us strive to be—navigating through the world, taking care of the people we love, and always using our powers for good. (Also, who doesn't want a sassy talking cat?) Sure, sometimes she makes things really weird for a day at school, but she knows how to forgive herself and apologize, and that's strong magic indeed.

WITCH: Sarah Bailey
SKILL: Bravery
The Craft's Sarah Bailey is a witch who understands that right choices are not always easy to make. She easily could have followed her coven into reckless and harmful magic, but instead she fights against them, even when they try to use her mental health struggles against her.

WITCHES: The Witches of Eastwick
SKILL: The power of the coven
Is there any better story than one where three powerful women discover they're better off without a toxic man? We think not. The Witches of Eastwick are indeed manipulated by a man, but they grow to understand they're stronger together. Their story is the ultimate triumph of female friendship. And, of course, Cher is the best.

· CHAPTER ·

2

GLAMOURS

THE POWER TO CHANGE HOW YOU LOOK

It's no coincidence that *glamour*—the term for an appearance-changing charm in early English tales of witches and fairies—has become a modern word denoting charisma, beauty, and élan. Appearance can be magic, and powerful magic at that. But instead of casting shape-shifting spells, we can experiment with new makeup, bold outfits, and rebellious hairstyles.

Changing your appearance might sound simple or shallow. In fact, it's anything but. Society tells women that devoting oneself to beauty and fashion is at once obligatory (otherwise we look unforgivably hideous), a silly waste of time (appearance is inherently superficial), and deceptive (see: men posting memes about makeup as "betrayal" and "the reason you have to take a woman swimming on the first date"). But within these crazily contradictory expectations lies the root of glamorous power: beauty is something that women alone are expected to perform, involving mysterious rituals, talismans, and bottled potions, which can influence an observer's perception to the point of being almost menacing. It sounds like the beauty arts are scoffed at precisely *because* they make women powerful.

In reality, you're not deceiving people when you indulge in cosmetic shape-shifting. You're not being shallow, either. Rather, you're letting your true self shine through. You're slogging out from the mire of messages about acceptable appearances and discovering how you want to look—perhaps not by magically changing your hair color à la Nymphadora Tonks, but by learning how to manipulate and enhance your self-image using makeup, hair, and clothing. Whether you draw strength from unusual lipstick colors, an all-black outfit, or a lucky amulet, this chapter will help you discover how to look and feel more like yourself.

How to Clothe Yourself in Literal Darkness

YOU DON'T HAVE TO WEAR ALL BLACK TO WITCH HERE, BUT IT HELPS

〰〰

The first step in casting off beauty ideals is to return to a blank slate. And by blank slate, we mean *black* slate. Because if witches know one thing, it's the power of the color black. Black clothes, black hats, black cats, black chokers, black nails, black lips, black magic.

Why black clothes? Take your pick: black is good for standing out, but it's also good for blending in. (Think of spies or cat burglars—basically, if your job involves doing secret things at night, this is your color.) All-black outfits can be chic, punk, businesslike, bohemian, dressy, or devil-may-care. You'll almost never look out of place in black (unless you're at a wedding, and even that taboo has started to fade, probably because so many people's go-to dresses these days are black). In Western countries, black is associated with death and mourning, so by wearing the color of death, you project a kind of fearlessness. And, sure, people say black is "slimming," but really, black is the color of *vast* things: the night sky, the deep earth, the inside of your head when you close your eyes. In a way, wrapping yourself in black brings you close to infinity. Plus, it doesn't show dirt and it matches *everything*.

Unless you are working as a stagehand or attending a funeral, you don't *have* to wear black. But if you've never walked out the door in head-to-toe midnight, you ought to give it a try. Put a little bit of power, vastness, mutability, and doom into your wardrobe, and see how you feel! Here are a few tips for easing yourself into the all-black sisterhood.

▸ ▸ ▸ Take baby steps.

If black seems too intense but you still want to cast dark, witchy vibes out into the world, start by incorporating other dark colors into your wardrobe. Deep purples, blues, silvers, and grays all evoke the night sky, and nothing says "don't mess with me or I'll feed you a poison apple" like blood red. And if all-over black feels too flat for your aesthetic, find black clothing with a bit of shimmer or sparkle or pattern.

▸ ▸ ▸ Play with proportion.

Massive black robes might make you look like a witch, or like a nun. Instead, try pairing a long black skirt with a black camisole, or black jeans with a black crop top, or a black sweater with black shorts. (Unless you like the nun look, in which case absolutely go for it.)

▸ ▸ ▸ Mix textures.

Black-on-black patterns and textured fabrics—lace, embossed velvet, sheer, jacquard, tonal stripes—can fit any style from goth to chic, and a little goes a long way. Plus, having clothing in a variety of textures can save you from the witch's primary sartorial challenge: spotting the one black garment you're looking for in your pile of all-black clothing.

▸ ▸ ▸ Keep black clothes beautiful.

To prevent fading, wash black duds in cold water using a detergent specially designed for darks. Extend time between washings of black jeans by placing them in a plastic bag in the freezer to kill odors. Remove deodorant stains from black tops by wetting the area, covering it with salt, and letting it stand for a couple of hours before washing. And if your clothes do fade, don't drive yourself crazy digging for a slightly more faded pair of black leggings to wear with a slightly more faded top. Life's too short to match blacks. For a witch, it all counts.

▸ ▸ ▸ Curl up and dye.

There's no shortage of black clothing on the market, but making your own can be fun. Most craft stores sell black fabric dye, and although you can dye just about any garment, this is a good excuse for a shopping spree. Cool gloves, a vintage lace slip, or a luxurious shawl are easy to dye yourself. Plus, a vat of black liquid steaming on a stovetop is *pretty* close to a bubbling cauldron.

▶ ▶ ▶ Highlight with color.

Like the black velvet display case in a jeweler's window, your all-black outfit can serve as a background to set off whatever colorful gem you want people to focus on—whether that's a piece of jewelry, a tie, a bright hair color, a favorite hijab, a bold lipstick, or just the general gorgeousness of your face. Strategic use of black can command and direct attention as well as any spell does.

Now just grab your coordinating black cat, and take yourself out on the town.

Dress to Sorceress

HONING EMOTIONS
WITH MAGICAL OUTFITS

Every time you get dressed, you're putting on more than just a clean shirt: you're clothing yourself in an emotion, a persona, a sense of yourself. You're making a choice that affects how you'll move through the world. You probably have outfits that make you feel beautiful, handsome, or sexy, and totally different outfits that make you feel comfortable. You may even have certain items that feel like armor, such as cowboy boots, the perfect pencil skirt, or a favorite necktie. (Jess's is a motorcycle jacket; Jaya's is a pair of wedge sneakers covered in red glitter.) All these garments—your hot clothes, your comfy clothes, your armor clothes—not only make you feel a certain way as you wear them, but remind you how you felt wearing them in the past. What you wear affects your mindset and, consequently, the way you carry yourself. Although your clothes may alter your behavior in unconscious ways (think of how you automatically walk differently if you switch from combat boots to heels), you can actively engage the emotional power of clothing to change your mood.

Not all witches dress alike—Nancy from *The Craft* wouldn't be caught dead looking like Winifred from *Hocus Pocus*—so you can make clothing magic work within your personal style. Here are a few starting points for working simple spells every time you get dressed.

▶ ▶ ▶ For stability, wear flat or heavy shoes.

When you need to feel grounded, leave the stilettos at home and opt for sturdy platforms, wedges, ballet flats, or sneakers.

▶ ▶ ▶ For emotional protection, wear layers.

Having more than one thickness of fabric between you and the world makes for a safer, more armored feeling.

▶ ▶ ▶ For confidence, wear loud jewelry.

If you make yourself small and quiet in the presence of others, let your jewelry do the talking. Wear bangles that jingle and clang, anklets with bells, or rings that clink together when you move your fingers.

▶ ▶ ▶ For comfort in times of stress, wear soft, soothing textures.

By wearing fabrics you like to touch, like velvet, suede, or fleece, you can easily comfort yourself in stressful situations. Try a velvet dress on the first day of school, or a jersey skirt on a date, and rub the fabric between your fingers when you feel nervous.

▶ ▶ ▶ For relief from worry or fear, wear tight-fitting accessories.

Ever put a nervous dog in a Thundershirt? Same idea: a little (gentle!) pressure can help you focus on being present in your body, which activates the parasympathetic nervous system and quells anxiety. Try a cloth headband or wristband for stylish relief.

The more you use clothes to focus your emotional energy, the better you'll get at channeling a particular feeling whenever you need—the power has been in you all along. You may not be able to wear a motorcycle jacket everywhere—at certain weddings, for instance, or at most job interviews, or on the beach—but inwardly, you'll be wearing a *spiritual* motorcycle jacket, one that nobody can remove.

Makeup for Witches

GETTING THE "UNNATURAL" LOOK

Women are taught that makeup is best used sparingly, as an enhancement to one's natural features. And most makeup on the market reflects that attitude: lipsticks come in shades of pink, red, and various flesh tones; eyeshadows promise to "bring out the color" of your eyes; blush is tinted to play up the bloom in your cheeks, and mascara is designed to lengthen the lashes you already have. Study upon study shows that men do not like women who wear "too much" makeup, that they prefer women to look soft, unintimidating, and "natural."

But everything about makeup is unnatural. And that's why it can be so powerful.

Wearing cosmetics, whether tinted lip balm or full-on contouring, is just good, old-fashioned shape-shifting: you decide to change the way you look, and then you use tools at your disposal to do so. That's amazing. That's witchcraft. Rather than highlighting what others consider beautiful, you can emphasize what you think is beautiful, or weird, or scary, or whatever you want people to notice, and then use nontraditional color choices to achieve that effect. Red eyeshadow, blue mascara, and green lipstick are all just as good options as pinks and browns. Here's how to make the best use of makeup.

▸ ▸ ▸ Go back to black.

Unlike soft, pastel, or subtle cosmetics, all-black makeup is an extra-bold look and can banish your expectations about what a made-up face "should" look like. Paint on black lipstick (or apply liquid eyeliner to lips). Paint the entirety of your eyelids black and smudge it out as far as it'll go. Hell, use black eyeshadow as contouring bronzer. Even if you wear it for just a few minutes by yourself, let black makeup be a positive shock to your system (and snap a selfie while you're at it).

▸ ▸ ▸ Give yourself a magical color boost.

Enliven your palette by looking to the colors that witches traditionally associate with emotions or qualities. Reds grant strength and power; blues are all about tranquility and peace. Yellow connotes joy, green deals with luck (especially in finances), and purple signifies healing. (The signs of the zodiac are sometimes associated with specific hues, too.) Pair colors with facial features to further strengthen this magic. Want to channel female energy to your soul? Cover your eyelids in silver powder. Want to encourage kind words to come out of your mouth? Paint your lips orange. Want everything you touch to bring you financial success? Get yourself a green manicure.

▸ ▸ ▸ Make yourself look weird.

Abandon all pretense of "natural" in favor of scary, or silly, or dead serious. Instead of skin-tone bronzer, dust your cheeks with a wild color of eyeshadow, like dark blue, or bright purple, or neon green. Swap your usual blood-red lipstick with yellow, orange, or white. Sprinkle on glitter, or try affixing skin-safe sequins with cosmetic adhesive around your eyes. Take eyeliner way outside your lashline. Swipe colorful mascara on your lashes *and* your brows. Then observe your look and how you feel about it. What are the things you like about your face, not because you've been told they're traditionally beautiful, but just because you like them? Pushing the boundaries of what makeup "should" look like pushes back on society's expectations. But more than that, it helps you discover your own personal definition of sexy, pretty, or attractive.

▶ ▶ ▶ Get naturally unnatural with DIY makeup.

If you want to truly feel like a witch mixing up potions, whip up your own makeup at home—it's easier than you'd think, and you can control exactly what goes into it (and, therefore, onto you). Any homemade makeup consists of either a liquid base (for things like lip tints, cream blushes, or eyeliner) or a neutral powder base (for powder foundations, blush, and bronzer), plus coloring ingredients. Common liquid bases include coconut oil and petroleum jelly, and arrowroot powder is a popular powder base. For color tints, anything nontoxic and safe to eat is fair game, but avoid inflammatory substances—like ground cayenne powder!—in your mixture. If you're not sure whether your makeup might irritate you, apply a small amound to the inside of your wrist as a patch test before getting close to eyes or lips.

MAKEUP RECIPES

Loose bronzer: Mix arrowroot powder with ground cinnamon and cocoa powder. (If you prefer bronzer set in a compact, add a few drops of coconut or jojoba oil to make it stick together.)

Lightly tinted lip balm: Mix beet root powder and coconut oil. For a thicker, more deeply pigmented lip color, add food coloring and beeswax.

Natural black mascara: Combine activated charcoal with coconut oil and aloe vera.

Find Your Colors

Lots of beauty brands will try to match "flattering" colors to your skin tone or eyes, but what are the colors that are going to make you feel as beautiful and enchanting as possible?

WHAT YOU'LL NEED:

A full moon

A bathtub

A candle in your favorite color

Matches

Draw a warm bath and light the candle at the edge of the tub. Stare into the flame as you recite this incantation three times:

Fire, earth, water, sea
Let the rainbow shine through me.

Repeat the incantation silently as you close your eyes, and picture yourself from above. Visualize your body, and then watch the water around you slowly change color. It could be all one color or a few. Then let the color or palette you see inspire your makeup looks—even if it's a shade you've always been told not to wear. Be as bold or subtle as you like; if you see blue, for instance, you could go for retro blue eyeshadow, striking ice-blue lips, or even a classic blue-toned red.

If you (like Jess) hate baths, you can also find your spirit colors by meditating. Close your eyes and picture yourself in a room where you feel a profound sense of ease and safety. You are sitting in an armchair, and there is a flower in a vase. Concentrate on your feeling of security, then look at your surroundings. What color is the upholstery? The flower? The quality of the light in the room?

Now envision yourself outside, in a setting of transcendent beauty. You're surrounded by flowers here, too, and the scenery is so spectacular it almost takes your breath away. Concentrate on that feeling of overpowering beauty and then look around. What color are the flowers? What color is the sky?

These visualizations help you tap into the colors you associate with different mental states and thoughtfully incorporate them into your makeup and wardrobe in order to feel gorgeous or invincible.

WITCH HISTORY

WHEN WEARING MAKEUP
MADE YOU A WITCH

ACCORDING TO A POPULAR myth, married women in Britain were once legally banned from wearing lipstick, on pain of having their marriages annulled and being accused of witchcraft. In reality, no such law existed (or if it did, no historian has found proof of it), but its persistence as an urban legend reveals the extent of society's deep distrust of makeup. Many people can believe that lipstick was once not just a tool of beauty, but a tool of the devil.

In fact, in addition to rumors, some real historical laws have linked lipstick and sorcery. According to lipstick historian Jessica Pallington, in medieval England "a woman who wore make-up was seen as an incarnation of Satan" because she was changing the face God gave her. However, wealthy women at the time were hiring alchemists to whip up lipsticks for them while chanting incantations, and evidently Satan's rules didn't apply to the rich. By the 1500s, Catholic women were told to mention lipstick use in confession. In the 1700s in America, a man could have his marriage annulled if his wife had worn cosmetics during courtship—although in France at that time, going bare-faced was considered acceptable only for prostitutes. Go figure.

Before the advent of commercially manufactured cosmetics, part of the suspicion regarding makeup was the effect some ingredients had on the wearer. Rouge for cheeks and white powder foundation were made with lead and mercury, which could eat at skin. Women dripped belladonna (aka deadly nightshade) into their eyes to make them appear big and seductive. Given the occasional dangerous (and sometimes lethal) ingredient and makeup's ability to camouflage one's appearance, no wonder it was considered so witchy.

Even after the age of literal witch hunts, makeup remained a lightning rod for issues of politics, class, and morality. By the 1910s in America, bright red lipstick became a symbol of defiance and women's emancipation, as retaliation against cosmetics often being sold under the counter. Elizabeth Cady Stanton and Charlotte Perkins Gilman wore red lipstick at the 1912 New York City Suffragette March to show that they meant business. As the look gained popularity, lipstick was seen as so terrifying that it was almost banned by the male officials of the New York Board of Health in 1924 for fear that women would use it to poison them (you know, like a witch would).

No matter the historical era, at the heart of any makeup controversy has always been the fear of feminine dishonesty. Every argument against cosmetics, whether anger that they give women power to enhance their appearance or outrage that they allow women to call attention to themselves, boils down to men not wanting women to be in control of their own bodies. Which, unfortunately, many men still don't want. Stanton and Gilman wore red lips to protest more than a hundred years ago, but lipstick still has the power to confuse, annoy, and terrify. We see no reason to stop now.

NAIL ART TO TERRIFY MEN

Stiletto nails

Coffin nails

Buzzsaw nails

Spiderweb manicure

Poison nails

Cauldron nails

"Non-applicator tampon" manicure

"I'm not listening to you" manicure

Excess body hair manicure

Emotions manicure

Nails in the silhouettes of feminist icons

Undone nails

Wear Bold Lipstick

*This spell helps you feel
beautiful and self-assured while
defying beauty standards—
something ordinary pink lip tint
can never give you.*

WHAT YOU'LL NEED:

A cheap tube
of bright lipstick

A red candle

A safety pin
or small knife

Matches

Growing up, Jaya was always timid about bright lipsticks. She thought they'd only draw unwanted attention to her lips, which felt awkward and too large for her face. But change came in the form of lavender lipstick she spotted at the makeup store. At first she thought *this shouldn't work*. Surely it would wash her out, or clash with her undertones, or do something that makeup experts thought was wrong for her face. But she tried it on anyway.

Maybe the makeup experts were right. It didn't emphasize her coloring or do her undertones any favors. It looked weird—but then it looked *awesome*. Looking at her reflection, she realized she actually liked her lips and could wear whatever she wanted on them. All she had to do was summon the confidence.

Wash your face so that it is free of all makeup. Apply the lipstick to your clean lips. Then, in the middle of your chest, draw a swirl using the lipstick. Make it as big as you can (maybe you strip down to your bra for this), then draw swirls on your arms, legs, neck, and all over your body until you're covered, or until you run out of lipstick. Reserve the tube—you'll need it later.

With the safety pin, carve your name into one side of the candle and a pair of lips into the other side. Kiss the lips you carved, place the candle in a fireproof dish, and light it with the match. Staring into the flame, recite the following:

My lips are mine
My lips are free
My lips will look how I want them to be

Close your eyes and picture your face, remembering those words. Sit that way for as long as you like. Let the candle burn down until the flame dies, and take a shower. After you've washed off all the lipstick, keep the image of yourself wearing it in your mind's eye. Carry the empty tube in your purse or backpack for a week afterward.

The Dark Magic of
Unfeminine Haircuts

In recent years, the notion of so-called ideal beauty has shifted. Although ideas of what makes a woman beautiful still skew white and Western, American society has started to accept (a little) variation in terms of whether women should be plump or thin, short or tall, dark or pale. But one thing is compulsory: long hair. Sure, the pixie cut enjoys an occasional fashion moment, but usually this style is lauded as part of an androgynous look rather than a feminine one. Perfect femininity—whatever that is— still requires long, smooth, flowing locks.

Thankfully, we witches cackle in the face of perfect femininity. We aren't interested in conforming to standards so much as triumphantly watching people squirm when the standards are destroyed. Your witchy hairdo can be an engine for confidence and power—power that comes from you alone, not from your ability to mimic ideals. It can also be a signal to other unruly women that you're part of their coven—that you're daring, unconventional, and uninterested in traditional femininity.

If you have Disney princess tresses and love them, of course, by all means keep them—but, no matter what *Little Women* taught you, never believe that your hair is not "your one beauty." This isn't true, and even if it were, you don't owe your beauty to anyone. If you're looking to break out of the hair box (wow, does that ever sound like a gross euphemism), here are a few types of hairstyle magic to consider.

▶ ▶ ▶ Shaved head

The shaved head is a banishing spell. It's a total elimination of the concept of hair as accessory—with a shaved head, your face is what you get. Shaving your head is a drastic change, and you risk learning the hard way that your skull is a weird shape. But weigh that against the prospect of freeing yourself from one of the million things women are supposed to worry about.

How to do it: Talking a stylist into shaving your head can be hard—there's no going back with this 'do! But it's not too hard to DIY, if you have the courage. First cut your hair short with scissors, then have a friend use an electric clipper over your whole head. Start with a long guard on the clipper and see how it looks; you can always go shorter. And don't forget: your head now needs sunscreen, even more than the rest of you!

▶ ▶ ▶ Undercut/side shave

The partial shave is a hex on expectations. You have options with this cut: Shave the side! Shave both sides! Shave the underside all the way around your head! Shave everything but your bangs! (Technically this last one is called a Chelsea cut, not an undercut, but this distinction matters only when you go to the salon and ask for it. We include it here as a variation of "partly shaved, partly not.") In some ways, a partial shave is even more subversive than a full buzz cut: instead of doing away with feminine tresses entirely, you're cutting into them, mutilating them. "Here's what I think of your beauty standards," this style says. (Also, it's well ventilated in the summer, and with it you kinda look like Tank Girl.)

How to do it: We recommend enlisting a stylist, especially for maintenance between cuts, which can be tricky. Shave whichever side you prefer.

If you're bold enough to give yourself this look, start shaving from where your hairline meets your ear up to the parietal ridge, located about three finger-widths above the top of the ear (you should be able to feel a bony ridge on your head where your skull starts to curve), although shaving the entire side can look great, too. How far back you shave, or whether you continue all the way around from one side to the other, depends on your preferences and your courage. (A three-quarters-around undercut can look weird, but sometimes weird is good!) If you plan to shave more than an inch or two behind your ear, ask a friend to wield the clipper. Start small—a long guard on the clipper, not shaving too much—and remember: you can always shave more but can't go back.

▶ ▶ ▶ Pixie cut

The pixie is a binding spell, combining apparent opposites: a boy's haircut and an iconic look in women's fashion. It's androgynous in a calculated way that says "I am stealing the power of Sexy Manhood and Sexy Womanhood at once." Stylists and fashion magazines, which typically subscribe to and reinforce that ol' thin white cisgender beauty ideal, might advise against attempting the pixie unless you have every other classical marker of feminine beauty (a thin body, high cheekbones, big eyes, full lips, whatever). But we encourage you to harness the powers of the pixie—versatility, liminality, *really really easy* maintenance—no matter your face, form, or gender presentation.

How to do it: Do not DIY this look—it's much more complicated than running clippers over your head! Go to a salon (with a stylist who specializes in short hair if possible), and bring pictures of what you'd like. Ask for a look that's a little shorter than you think you want, especially in the back of your head, because hair tends to grow in fast; if it's too long near your neck, that's your ticket to mullet city. (The mullet is, of course, a legit look—see below—but if you want a pixie, it probably isn't what you're going for!) If the stylist says that you "don't have the face" for a pixie, pack up and take your business elsewhere.

▶ ▶ ▶ Asymmetrical cut

The asymmetrical haircut is an illusion spell, changing your look from every angle. You're not just one thing, so why should your hair be? Like the undercut, this style contains multitudes: shorter on one side, longer on the other à la Tegan and Sara; short in the back with long wisps in the front à la Ramona Flowers; or even the classic mullet. This 'do is a radical embracing of duality. Attempt it when you've learned, or want to learn, to love your contradictions.

How to do it: This is another look that's best achieved with the help of a professional. Bring the stylist pictures of the haircut you've envisioned, but also ask what kind of look will work for your hair length and texture.

Don't forget practical considerations of your new 'do—for instance, will half your hair now be too short to put up in a ponytail? Can you live with that, or do you need to tweak your plan?

▸ ▸ ▸ Natural hair

Natural hair is a shape-shifting spell, says writer and beauty expert Hannah Giorgis. "There's this idea that to be marked feminine is to have your hair straight or as close to white women's as possible," she says—which means that by embracing your natural texture, if it's anything other than smooth and straight, you're giving the finger to stereotypes. Although Hannah does not personally feel like "I'm reclaiming my blackness" through her natural hair, some women do have this experience. She does feel, however, that her hairstyle keeps her in touch with herself in a purely practical way, through the practice of self-care. Having to slow down and spend time with her hair, she says, "can be really restorative and a space for reflection."

How to do it: The process of growing out a perm depends on your hair's texture, how long you've been chemically relaxing your hair, and the look you're going for, says Hannah. Accordingly, she recommends watching YouTube tutorials from people whose texture matches your own: "There's a huge community to immerse yourself in, so it's not a solitary experience now as it might have been years ago." Also consider taking baby steps. "I personally recommend growing your hair out for a little bit, chopping it off, and doing braids," she says. "You can kind of ease your way into it." And remember, it's just a shape-shifting spell. "The body can always be altered."

If anyone weeps about you ruining your one beauty, remind them that your beauty is too vast to be contained in a mere hundred thousand strands of collagen. Besides, beauty isn't just something you *have*; it's something you *do*. The power of glamour comes from manifesting the exact image you want. Any hairstyle that creates positive feelings is beautiful.

A SPELL FOR

Haircut Confidence

*Even if you're ready for a change,
a drastic haircut can be a leap of faith.
This spell can help settle your mind
before you head to the salon.*

WHAT YOU'LL NEED:

Scissors
(smaller is better)

2 pieces of tape

Use the scissors to snip a small lock of hair from a hidden spot on your head. Tape one end of the strand to a table or counter. Stroke the strand seven times, focusing your mind on your anxieties: What's the worst-case scenario for this haircut? What are your worries about your appearance? What are you frightened people will think of you?

Carefully separate the piece of hair into three parts, and plait it into a simple braid. As you braid, picture your anxieties being tangled and trapped into the pattern. Each time you cross one strand over another, more of your worries are caged inside the braid and away from your conscious mind.

Tape the end of the braid. Remove the taped end from the table and fold it over to hold the other end of the braid. Hold the braid between your hands, close to your heart. Thank your hair for having been a part of you, and for carrying your anxieties away with it.

Bury the hair in a flowerpot or in the ground, or loop it around a branch of a tree or bush to release your anxieties into nature.

The Power of a Good Talisman

If you've ever believed in the power of a favorite necklace, a lucky ring, or even a pair of underwear you wear every time you have a date, you've channeled the magic of the talisman. And if you haven't, maybe you want to.

A talisman is an object imbued with a beneficial magical property, usually luck or protection. The protective strength of a talisman can come from the symbolic power of its form, or from a charging ritual, or both. Wearing or carrying a talisman allows it to work its magic on you and reminds you of the magic you carry within.

Talismans aren't just for witches, either. Endowing objects with meaning beyond their practical use is already part of modern life, but the magical symbolism has become invisible to most of us. A wedding ring, for example, is just a band of metal. But on someone's hand it becomes a signal to society—it's a marker, physical proof of the kind of relationship most of us believe is powerful and sacred. Wearing a wedding ring is not a requirement if you're married, nor is it against the law for you to wear a ring on your fourth finger if you're single: the power of the wedding ring comes from the meaning ascribed by the person wearing it and their culture. (Remember in the film *Practical Magic* when Sally attempts to explain magic to her romantic interest, the policeman? "Your badge," she says, taking it in her hand, "it's just a star, just another symbol. Your talisman. It can't stop criminals in their tracks, can it? It has power because you believe it does.")

An object need not have cultural significance to have personal significance, however—anything you wear or carry can be a talisman, and its symbolism doesn't have to be overt. An heirloom, a long-held favorite item of clothing, or any piece of jewelry you find visually or emotionally appealing can work to boost your confidence, calm your nerves, or remind you to care for yourself. Pick a talisman because it's in your favorite color, or its shape is comforting and familiar, or it symbolizes your interests and desires. You can use something you already own or shop for something new, as long as the piece speaks to you. Classic charms in witchy shapes like stars, crescent moons, cats, and cauldrons can remind you of your dark power, or else you can have a pendant or bracelet custom engraved with a specific word or phrase that keeps you centered.

TRADITIONAL POWERS OF STONES AND GEMS

Amethyst: Healing and protection against negative energy

Moonstone: Balance and enhancement of the feminine

Turquoise: Grounding emotions and opening the heart

Jade: Good luck, fortune, and longevity

Opal: Amplifying emotions and feelings, especially those of love and passion

Rose quartz: Promoting gentleness, peace, and calm

So whether it's your vintage turquoise pendant that makes you feel grounded, your grandmother's pearl ring reminding you that you come from a line of strong women, or that one T-shirt you were wearing when you got an A on a math test, pick a talisman that makes you feel lucky, protected, or powerful. Listen to your intuition; pick what gives you good vibes, and the rest will follow. The magic works only if you believe it, like Sandra Bullock taught us, and your talisman is a reminder of what you have.

Once you've selected a potential talisman, all you need to do is imbue it with a concentrated version of the feeling you want to invoke. The simplest way to charge a talisman is through visualization: hold the object and focus intensely on an image of yourself at your most happy, fortunate, productive, or loved. But a more effective—and almost certainly more fun—method is to do it for real. This just requires a little creativity.

Think of a way to induce a small, pure example of the feeling that you want to endow your talisman with. Take the object with you as you experience this feeling, and when the emotion is at its peak, imagine it as a light streaming out of you and flowing into the item, being held there permanently.

IDEAS FOR TALISMAN-CHARGING ADVENTURES

For happiness: Ride a roller coaster, eat a sundae, have an orgasm.

For strength: Lift a heavy weight, scale a climbing wall, crush something safe to crush (nutshells, tin cans).

For serenity: Float in water, watch a sunset, pet a dog.

For confidence: Have an orgasm. (Orgasms will work for almost any of these, let's be real.)

Think creatively and personally: you can do anything that reliably makes you feel happy, peaceful, confident, or whatever experience you want to catch and bottle. When you wear or look at your talisman in the future, you'll remember charging it with the essence of that energy, and you'll be able to feel it again. Like Dumbo with his feather, the ability to fly was in you all along! Go forth with your talisman, and let power radiate from you.

The Secret Art
of Smellomancy

~~~

Every year, ladies' magazines from *Glamour* to *Allure* to *Elle* offer tips on how to find your "signature scent." (Buzzfeed and the Victoria's Secret website offer online quizzes for this, if magazines aren't your thing.) Signature scents are cool, of course—if you always wear the same perfume, people in your life probably think of you whenever they smell it. But what if you could use your scent to make *you* think of you—the best version of you, the you that you need to be at this exact moment? What if you could use your scent to evoke your strengths and skills?

This form of magic—we call it smellomancy—draws on the powerful connection between smell and memory. The part of the brain that processes scents and smells (the olfactory bulb) is located near the parts of the brain associated with memories and emotions (the hippocampus and amygdala), and your sense of smell has the unique power to tap into this part of your mental makeup. You can learn to evoke a particular mental state by wearing a scent that you associate with that feeling. Throughout the day, the fragrance will subtly evoke the time you felt most powerful, most attractive, most secure, most unusual. And, like the tiny molecules of your perfume wafting up from your skin and getting stuck in people's noses, you'll project that feeling to everyone you meet.

▶ ▶ ▶ **Choose a scent.**

You don't need expensive perfumes for this—you can find smells that feel right to you without dropping a lot of dough. Many perfume-sellers on Etsy are happy to provide samples, and makeup stores or high-end drugstores often will let customers spritz a bunch of fragrances on strips of paper and sniff them. For a more natural option, try bottled essential oils sold at an herb store or an organic market, or even combine oils and mix your own custom blend. Wherever you find it, make sure the smell speaks to you.

▶ ▶ ▶ Map smells onto feelings.

To charge your scent with a specific positive emotion, wear it in situations that are virtually guaranteed to evoke that particular feeling. Wear your "comfort" smell to watch your favorite show, your "confident" smell for a test you know you're going to nail, or your "strong" smell to the gym. Don't jump right into wearing your "attractive" smell on a date; instead, first apply it when going out in your favorite outfit with your most complimentary friend.

POWERFUL SCENTS TO TRY

For happiness: frankincense, lemon, and grapefruit

For mental acuity: rosemary, lemon, and jasmine

For strength and vigor: peppermint

For calm and comfort: orange, vanilla, and lavender

For creativity: vanilla and cinnamon

For attractiveness: black licorice, lavender, and pumpkin pie spice (really)

▶ ▶ ▶ Use your newly charged potion.

With different flavors of positive energy bound up in each scent, you can apply your attitude like you apply moisturizer. Spritz on your fragrance whenever you need a boost, and the smell will provide little reminders of the way you want to feel all day.

Dapper Magic

"But guys," you may be saying, "I don't want to wear *any* makeup, unnatural or otherwise, and I prefer a masculine gender presentation—beauty tips aren't for me!"

That's cool! All are welcome in the coven, and deliberately calibrating your self-presentation is magic whether you're wearing a skirt or slacks. If you're masculine-presenting—which could mean you're a man, a woman who favors a butch look, or somewhere else on the gender spectrum—you can use the magic of paints and potions to influence your self-confidence and the way others perceive you. Biology isn't destiny—your assigned sex at birth isn't your gender—but identity isn't destiny either, and being masculine-of-center doesn't prohibit you from dabbling in the magical arts of performed femininity. After all, femininity is always a performance—no one is born knowing how to use makeup. Through exposure to the rituals like mascara application and leg shaving and accessorizing artfully, we figure out what it means to be "feminine." We can choose to emulate or subvert femininity; either way, these rituals can become part of our witchcraft toolkit.

If paints and powders aren't your thing, you can harness the power of glamours in plenty of gender-nonconforming ways. Consider these options.

▶ ▶ ▶ Use your power colors.

Remember when you discovered which colors make you feel relaxed, or strong, or attractive? Those are by no means just for makeup. Incorporate the colors that evoke your preferred mood through a shirt, a tie, a pocket square, cool socks, a watchband, or even a semipermanent hair color.

▶ ▶ ▶ Embrace the darkness.

Yes, you *can* wear all-black menswear without looking like an undertaker or a hit man. The key is to mix textures. Wear a blazer with a bit of sheen over a soft black sweater, or pair your suit with a vest, shirt, and/or tie that features a subtle black-on-black pattern. Match shiny black with matte black, smooth with textured.

▸ ▸ ▸ Put the *man* in talisman.

Talismans don't have to be girly jewelry. Anything portable that you can keep on your person is a potential talisman, except something that might get a lot of incidental use, such as a handkerchief. Try turning a solid accessory like a pocket watch, tie clip, key ring, or simple leather cuff into your holder of power.

▸ ▸ ▸ Mix up your smellomancy.

Try channeling positive emotions into traditionally masculine fragrances like sandalwood, vetiver, and leather. Don't wear cologne? A nicely scented body wash, deodorant, or shaving cream can store emotional power.

Reject Pressure to Be Feminine

Perform this charm to symbolically free yourself from society's expectations and insulate yourself against the demands of others.

WHAT YOU'LL NEED:

Newspaper, cardboard, or other material to protect work surface

2 sheets of white paper

A tube of pink or red lipstick (not gloss), organic if you can afford it

A pen with blue, black, or your favorite color ink

As we've shown in this chapter, you can engage with the magic of self-care and self-presentation in plenty of ways without even dipping a toe in femininity. But given the strength of societal pressures to conform, you might want this extra boost.

Spread the newspaper over the work surface and place a sheet of paper on top. With the lipstick, write on the paper all the ways you've been pressured to express femininity. Include any hurtful things people have said to you for not being a girl or not being more girly. Don't be dainty—scrawl. Make a mess. Press hard. (Don't worry if you go off the edges of the paper. That's what the newspaper is for.) Use the entire tube, but save the container. Then fold the paper seven times and bury it under a bush or tree, in a flowerpot, or, if necessary, among organic waste (such as vegetable peels) in your trash can. As the paper breaks down, those burdens will feed beauty—just not yours. Yours comes from somewhere else.

On the second sheet of paper, use the pen to write all the ways in which you want to be seen. List what makes you feel valuable, successful, attractive, and loved. Fold the paper three times, roll it into a tube, and slide it into the empty lipstick container. Sleep with the container under your pillow for three nights.

Lotions and Potions

~~~

Even if you've never picked up an eyeliner pencil and never will, you can tap into the power of glamours by helping your skin look its best. Try these makeup-free beauty rituals to feel more grounded, happy, protected, and at home in your body.

▶ ▶ ▶ Sunscreen for protection
Apply sunscreen, or a sun-protecting moisturizer or BB cream, daily. Picture the sunscreen creating a bubble of safety, shielding you from casual damage or danger.

▶ ▶ ▶ Sheet masks for transfiguration
Ordinary versions of these facial masks make the wearer look like a freaky ghost or mummy, but now you can get ones that are printed with the image of a panda, tiger, dragon, or even Cleopatra. Use them to soothe and moisturize your face while also getting in touch with your inner animal (or queen of ancient Egypt).

▶ ▶ ▶ Moisturizer for manifestation
Hydrating lotion that has a pleasant scent is a treat for the senses, and using it is an excellent way to feel strong and secure in your body. Apply it slowly, taking time to appreciate every part of your body as both a source and receiver of appealing touch, looks, and fragrance. (A smooth lotion or oil works best; occlusives like Vaseline are too thick.)

▶ ▶ ▶ Cleanser for tabula rasa
It sounds like a marketing campaign, but washing your face before bed truly can feel like rinsing away the stresses of the day. Cleansing your face doesn't have to be a multistep process, with toner and serum and whatnot, but let it be a conscious, meditative experience of renewal, rather than a perfunctory habit you do on autopilot simply so you don't get zits.

▸▸▸ Shaving (or not shaving) for conviction

The question of whether women should remove hair, and how much, and from where, is a vexing one. The two of us can't (and don't want to) tell you that you must shave your armpits or wax your mustache, but we can't (and don't want to) tell you that you must *not* do it, either. Letting your body hair grow free could feel like the epitome of unruliness, like giving a little up-yours to a society that wants us polished and pristine. But perhaps the unruliest option of all is to throw away notions of what you "should" do and instead do whatever makes you feel best. That might mean removing hair, letting it grow, or removing it only from the places where you don't like it. If you remove some, use the time you spend doing so as an opportunity to consciously reflect on how you want your body to look and feel. And if you don't remove hair, take a moment every so often to revel in its lushness and texture. Appreciating your hair or smooth skin, rather than reacting to other people's expectations, will allow you to feel the strength of your own beliefs glowing inside you.

When picking products, don't be afraid to splurge; using fancy moisturizers or face masks containing ingredients like gold or pearl will allow you to envision yourself as valuable. No need to break the bank, though. Affordable, natural skincare products can root you in the nurturing power of the earth. Try the appropriately named witch hazel as toner, sweet almond oil as a face cleanser, grape seed extract to fight wrinkles, tea tree oil or grapefruit seed extract to treat acne, and coconut oil for literally anything (makeup remover, body moisturizer, hair mask). Consider decanting skin care products into beautiful witchy jars and bottles to transform your bathroom into an arcane apothecary.

Self-Care

This quick, gender-neutral ritual charges up your preferred moisturizer, sunscreen, aftershave, or other personal care product (even deodorant, if you like).

WHAT YOU'LL NEED:

Any kind of daily or regular-use product

A blank white sticker or mailing label

A pen

Find a quiet, safe place with no distractions. Close your eyes and envision the version of yourself that feels most handsome, beautiful, or vibrant—however you like to feel. This could be realistic or not; if you feel best as a lizard person in Renaissance garb, we won't judge.

Picture your ideal self placing your hands together and a glow emanating from between them. Then, in your vision, open your hands and see that the glow surrounds a symbol, a simple combination of circles and lines. This symbol represents your ideal self.

Open your eyes, and draw the symbol you envisioned on your sticker. Affix the sticker to your bottle of moisturizer, sunscreen, or other product, imagining the glow you previously envisioned coming from your hands now permeating its contents.

Your product is now charged with the essence of whatever makes you feel strong and attractive. Every time you use it, picture that glow, and know that you're invoking the power and protection of your ideal self. The spell will last until you finish the product.

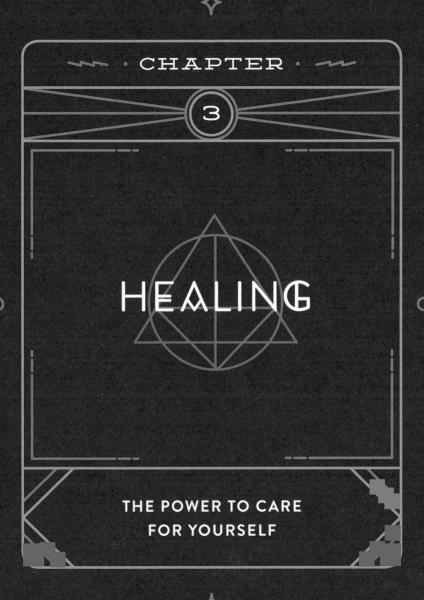

· CHAPTER ·

3

HEALING

THE POWER TO CARE
FOR YOURSELF

Taking care of yourself is not a revolutionary concept. But for many women nowadays, even the loving, sustaining maintenance of our own bodies is something we do for others. In our quest for the perfect waistline, the most glowing skin, or the best Runkeeper scores on Facebook, we prioritize *looking* healthy to others over genuinely feeling good. But when you divorce the pursuit of personal well-being from feelings of obligation and privation, self-care becomes something bigger than self-indulgence, and the pursuit of health goes from exhausting vigilance to invigorating celebration. Which is pretty magical.

The brewing and stewing of so-called witches of the past probably was not for summoning demons or enchanting unsuspecting layfolk to do their bidding. They likely were trying to keep each other healthy, and this tradition of healing and female-driven folk medicine may be where we get the myth of "women's intuition." Barred from formal medical or scientific training, female healers spread knowledge of cures and remedies to other women. Nowadays, we might dismiss this kind of homespun advice as innocuous "old wives' tales" or "home remedies," but squint, and it definitely resembles witchcraft—a potion of garden herbs that soothes contraction pains, a tea that stops an unbearable headache, and the intuition to give your body what it needs.

For a witch, listening to your body is the most important aspect of health and self-care—certainly more important than trying to whittle it into the "perfect" shape. Drowning out the whispering (or shouting) of a whole culture isn't easy, so when the noise gets to be too much, think about one of the healers of old—before the suspicion, before the witchcraft accusations, when she was just a woman with the skills and desire to help other women feel better. An intuitive woman, a traveling midwife, a woman wise in the body's ways. She wants you to be healthy. She will work to make it so. You can follow her.

In this chapter, we'll discuss how to use your powers to take care of yourself, whether that means accepting your body, finding exercises that make you feel invincible, or embracing the healing power of watching Netflix. Because sometimes that's the wisest thing you can do.

The Witch's Pantry

HOW TO CURE WHAT AILS YOU

~~~

We're fans of modern Western medicine. From vaccines to Pap smears to intrauterine devices, the products of medical research and empirical studies have made many lives better (and longer!) and improved public health overall. Needless to say, we hope you seek professional medical help when you're sick or think you might be sick, as well as for regular maintenance procedures like pelvic exams and management of any long-term conditions.

But as much as it has improved health generally, our medical culture doesn't work for everyone. Folks whose bodies or relationships to their bodies differ from the average—people who are very thin or even a little bit fat, people with disabilities or chronic illnesses, transgender people, and so forth—can feel especially unwelcome, unnerved, and misunderstood at doctors' offices. And though many physicians are kind, compassionate, and caring, medical schools and our healthcare system don't always reward or encourage those traits—plus doctors can be overworked and inattentive just like other humans.

Even when modern medicines work, sometimes side effects can be more debilitating than the original ailment or lead to a game of catchup: for instance, our friend Nicole told her doctor she didn't want to take a birth control pill because it made her depressed, so the doctor prescribed her an antidepressant. Had she complained of gaining weight on that antidepressant, she might have found herself with a prescription for Topamax, a migraine medication that is often prescribed to combat antidepressant-related weight gain. When you're taking pills to deal with the problems caused by pills you take to deal with the problems caused by pills, and you're not managing any kind of chronic or serious illness, it might be time to step back and get some perspective.

Making use of our modern medical establishment whenever needed is important, but it's also nice to treat milder symptoms the way wise woman healers might have done. Here's a tiny pharmacopeia of herbs and home remedies for when you're a touch under the weather.

▸ ▸ ▸ Aloe vera

An aloe plant is an even better kitchen multitasker than your combination grater/slicer/Microplane. This spiky succulent will look cute on your windowsill, and when disaster strikes, you can immediately break off a leaf and apply the juice to salve a burn or soothe a minor skin irritation. What's witchier than making a poultice out of your houseplant? (Aloe is a good moisturizer, too.)

▸ ▸ ▸ Ginger and peppermint

As tea, in candy, as essential oils, or in other preparations, ginger and peppermint have been shown to reduce nausea, even as a result of morning sickness (ginger) and irritable bowel syndrome (peppermint). Ginger is a more effective seasickness remedy than homeopathic spray, wrist bands, electric shocks on accupressure points, or a placebo (*MythBusters* confirmed it!).

▸ ▸ ▸ Cayenne

Once when Jess had a sinus infection, her boyfriend's mom made her snort a pinch of cayenne pepper. It hurt like hell, but also . . . kinda worked. Instead of snorting it, we recommend adding cayenne to your tea when you have a cold to fight congestion or combining cayenne, olive oil, and beeswax to make an analgesic salve (the capsaicin in the pepper reduces pain).

▸ ▸ ▸ Green tea

No, it probably doesn't prevent cancer or grant you the power to live to a hundred and twenty years old, or whatever, but green tea does have tons of antioxidant compounds called flavonoids, which can prevent cell damage and fight disease. Plus, a hot, healthful drink will leave you feeling alert, relaxed, and happy. Taking a few minutes to make a proper cup of tea—any kind—definitely counts as magical self-care.

▸ ▸ ▸ Witch hazel and tea tree oil

Witch hazel, which is widely available in drug stores, can be used as an astringent and toner to clean skin and prevent acne, and it might soothe itchy bug bites. Tea tree oil may help prevent acne, too, and take the edge off of bee stings. Sometimes witch hazel is used for more serious skin problems like eczema and psoriasis, and tea tree oil is sometimes recommended as an antifungal. As long as you're cautious (do not, for instance, take tea tree oil internally!) and willing to opt for a different remedy if things get worse, they might help and pose very little chance of harm.

▸ ▸ ▸ Turmeric

Sprinkle this anti-inflammatory spice in tea, or mix it with plain yogurt and a little honey and apply it as a face mask. Just don't leave it on your skin for too long—and *definitely* don't put it in a bath—unless you want to spend the rest of your life scrubbing an intense yellow stain off your face or tub (though if you do, lemon juice can help remove the discoloration). Also, according to Jaya's grandmother, warm milk with turmeric and a good night's sleep will cure any sickness you feel coming on. And Jaya's grandmother knows everything.

If you're combining herbal remedies with conventional medicine, double-check with your doctor or pharmacist about potential serious side effects—for example, St. John's wort, which has some clinical support as a natural treatment for depression, can also reduce the effectiveness of prescription medications (including birth control pills!). If your chosen herb is considered safe for you, the worst that can happen is nothing. And even if it does nothing, sometimes choosing to treat what's bothering you is enough to make you feel better on its own.

Feel Comfortable
Seeing a Doctor

Doctors can be intimidating, clinics can feel icky, and speaking up for yourself can be hard if you feel uncomfortable. This ritual draws out the part of you that is capable of confident self-advocacy.

WHAT YOU'LL NEED:

A small toy, stuffed animal, or figurine

Choose a stuffed animal, toy, action figure, or similar object that's small enough to fit in your purse or, if you don't carry one, your pocket. With your finger, draw a caduceus—that twisted-snakes emblem that indicates "medicine"—on the toy. Imagine light trailing your finger as you draw.

The toy is now your medical advocate. It wants you to feel healthy, but not at the expense of your emotional and mental stability. If you're uncomfortable or confused, or if you disagree with something the doctor is telling you, it will speak up for you. But because it is a toy, you'll have to speak on its behalf using your own words.

Bring your advocate with you to the appointment. (It doesn't have to leave your purse or pocket.) When the doctor tells you something, check in silently with your advocate: Did that make sense, or was it confusing? Is the doctor listening to me, or ignoring me? Is the way they're speaking to me respectful and kind, or brusque and dismissive? Do I feel welcome in this office? Does my gender appear correctly on the intake form? Are there blood pressure cuffs that fit my arm?

If at any point your advocate thinks your doctor is being too opaque, it will give you permission to ask for a clearer explanation. If your advocate thinks your doctor is wrong, it will give you permission to seek a second opinion. And if your advocate thinks you're being treated badly, it will give you permission to leave. Remember, it wants you to be healthy—but it will also stick up for you, even if you're too scared. Once your advocate gives you permission to do something, you can do it without fear, because you know you have a backup.

If you do need to leave, though, please tell the doctor "I don't feel comfortable with how you're treating me, and I'm going to leave now," and not "I'm taking advice from my capacity for confident self-advocacy, which I have projected into this Superman figurine." That could have unforeseen consequences.

WITCH HISTORY
WITCHES VS. DOCTORS

"THE HEALING AND HARMLESS witch must die," wrote William Perkins in his 1618 witch-hunting tome *Discourse of the Damned Art of Witchcraft*. Besides "those who kill and torment," he said, the righteous should seek to punish "all good Witches, which do no hurt but good, which do not spoil and destroy, but save and deliver." He drops the mic with the image of a harmless healer being put to death: "Death therefore is the just and deserved portion of the good Witch."

According to Perkins, healer witches were dangerous precisely *because* they were so beloved and vital. They performed a much-needed service for the community, and that distracted people from the fact that all witches had made a pact with the devil. How could you tell they'd made a pact with the devil? Why, because they possessed healing powers, of course.

The real source of their power was probably less satanic covenant and more actual knowledge. In *Witches, Midwives, and Nurses*, historians Barbara Ehrenreich and Deirdre English write that in ancient and medieval Europe, wise women were crucial, valued, beloved contributors to society who refined and administered effective folk remedies (including birthing, contraception, and abortions) for centuries with no issue. But once medicine became an exclusive, men-only academic profession around the thirteenth century, healer women were suddenly shunned as malign satanic influences.

The situation was a classic patriarchal double bind: women could be dragged to court for practicing medicine without having studied it, but they were also prohibited from studying medicine. Not that studying made you a more effective healer back then—quite the opposite, in fact. Where the wise women based their remedies in empirical observation, medieval universities taught based on theology and ancient texts—what worked was what Aristotle said worked hundreds of years ago, not techniques you'd effectively used to cure sick people. Here's a typical "witch" remedy, according to Ehrenreich and English: "Belladonna—still used today as an anti-spasmodic—was used by the witch-healers to inhibit uterine contractions when miscarriage threatened." Here's one from the schools: "A frequent treatment for leprosy was a broth made of the flesh of a black snake caught in a dry land among stones." But sure, fellas, your medicine sounds very special and good and not like magic at all.

These days, women are much better represented in academic medicine—a third of doctors and nearly half of medical students are women—but the Western medical establishment still sneers at folk remedies and midwifery. And yet empirical observation, so prized by today's physicians and scientists, has long been a hallmark of these hands-on traditions—noticing what works for which ailments is just the good old scientific method. Studies have found that, for healthy mothers, midwife-assisted births are less risky in several ways, and many alternative medicines have been shown to be effective (even if only as placebos). Is it too much to hope that folk traditions and established medical practices could be used together to keep people healthy? Maybe we should just celebrate that healing witches are no longer being put to death . . . which is definitely *not* a healthy decision.

Accept Compliments

WHAT YOU'LL NEED:

This spell will help you cultivate the confidence to be confident and believe in the radical power of your beauty. Perform it for your peace of mind or just to freak people out (both valid reasons).

A handheld mirror (larger is better, but a compact is fine)

A list of positive things about your face and body, written by a friend, partner, family member, or multiple people

In 2015, twenty-year-old Claire Boniface performed a social experiment: Whenever a man sent her a compliment on a dating website, she'd agree with it. The results were swift and startling—men instantly retracted or reversed the compliments as soon as she accepted them. (Here's a representative case: "Well you're bloody cute aren't ya," says an unnamed man. "Yes," says Boniface. "Not really," he snaps back.) When she shared the results on her Tumblr, the post went viral, and other women re-created the experiment to much the same results.

Gaining (or regaining) control over your self-confidence isn't easy—it feels almost out of your hands. Patriarchal culture needs women to stay anxious, on edge, and constantly seeking approval, and grants the power to *give* that approval to men only. But Boniface has given us words of power: Yes, I am. Thank you, I know. This spell builds on those simple, positive statements and can help incorporate loving (or not hating—baby steps!) your looks as a powerful part of your witchcraft practice.

Go outside on a clear day when the sun is high, ideally sometime between 10 a.m. and 2 p.m. Choose a quiet and peaceful outdoor spot where you feel at ease and where you'll be relatively alone. (If you live in a city, don't worry: people being a bit weird in public parks usually get a wide berth.) Find a spot to sit, or remain standing if you prefer.

Hold up the mirror with its nonreflective surface toward you and its reflective surface toward the sun, so that your face is in shadow. Say the first compliment on the list out loud: for instance, "you have beautiful eyes." You can say it under your breath if there are people around.

Slowly lower the mirror, turning it so that it reflects the light of the sun back up toward your face. (Don't look at the mirror! Just feel the light reflected on your skin.) Repeat the compliment, but this time in your own words: "I have beautiful eyes." As you say it, concentrate on the warmth of the sun. Imagine yourself soaking up the praise the way your skin soaks up warmth.

Repeat for each positive trait on the list. When you've completed the list, repeat the following three times:

I will not deflect.
I will reflect.

For the next two weeks, whenever you get a genuine compliment, lift and then lower your arm as if moving the mirror (if you are in private) or picture yourself making that motion (if you are in public). Imagine your skin feeling the warmth of the sun, and bask in the warmth of the praise. And then say "thank you."

Make Peace
with Your Body

WHAT YOU'LL NEED:

This spell combines various traditions of symbolic representation to foster an intuitive approach to repairing your relationship with your body.

Modeling clay

A pen or pencil

A sheet of paper

A sharp tool, such as an X-Acto knife or toothpick

The pin-filled, people-shaped pillows that Western society knows as voodoo dolls don't have much to do with the Haitian religious magical practice of vodou. But using little effigies for magic is a long-standing practice: witches in Europe were regularly accused of working malign spells using figures made of wax or cloth, and the ancient Egyptians would fill their tombs with small models of the servants, animals, and amenities they wanted to bring into the afterlife. In the case of this spell, you'll be pouring the magic into a figure that represents *you*.

Using the modeling clay, build a figure that represents the ideal body you've always thought you "should" have. (You can use Play-Doh, Sculpey, or homemade salt dough made with 1 part salt, 2 parts water, and 4 parts flour.) As you build, think about all the things you've denied yourself or thought you didn't deserve because of how your body looks. Think of all the things you would have done if you'd had a "perfect" body.

Close your eyes and smash the figure in your hands. Then start rolling it into a ball between your palms, keeping your eyes closed, and picture the ball beginning to glow with the concentrated essence of perfection and potential. Hold it in front of you, and picture it glowing brighter and brighter. On the face of the ball, imagine a symbol taking form. Open your eyes and draw that symbol on the paper so you don't forget it. If you don't see a symbol, just draw whatever comes into your head when you first open your eyes. This represents your ideal body, a body that can do whatever it wants.

Remodel the clay into a figure that looks like you—your actual body, the way it is today. Don't exaggerate, but also don't flatter: make it as detailed and realistic as possible. As you build, think again about what you would have done if you'd had a perfect body. Imagine yourself doing those things right now, with the body you have.

On every part of the figure that you dislike on your real body, use the sharp tool to draw the symbol you saw. Anoint every one of those parts with the symbol of perfection and potential, recognizing that you are capable as you are. You can use this incantation to focus your thoughts:

Only I can stop me
And I refuse to stop me
This is my body
This is a perfect body

Place the figure on top of, beneath, or near a mirror you use regularly. Leave it there for a week. Before each time you look in the mirror, touch the figure and imagine it glowing again.

Kitchen Witchery

NOURISH YOUR BODY AND
MIND WITH FOOD SPELLS

~~~

Chances are, if you're like most people, you practice a certain type of magic every day, several times a day. You apply forces to change the shape and texture of things. You fashion something new out of raw ingredients (sometimes with the aid of a literal bubbling cauldron). And eventually, you digest it and use it to create a new self. Yes, cooking is magic, even if all you did was microwave a frozen burrito.

Cooking doesn't come naturally to everyone, but no matter how simple or complicated your kitchen witching is, you can apply magic to it. Even if you're making something as simple as microwave popcorn for a friend, you can think about the good things in your friendship becoming even better with each pop, and voilà: magic. Whatever energy you give off is absorbed by the food, and then by whoever eats it. The effect may not be as immediate as in that terrible movie *Simply Irresistible*, where Sarah Michelle Gellar plays a witch who infuses emotion into her food (seriously, there's a magic crab in it or something), but there's no denying that food affects our feelings.

You can craft your kitchen adventures around specific ingredients, too, whether you use foods that are believed to have specific, semimagical properties—like the purported aphrodisiac effects of oysters, chocolate, pomegranates, and asparagus—or ordinary ingredients. Honey promotes love and wisdom. Garlic is used for health and protection. Dill is a powerful herb for intensifying whatever spell you're already using. And if you want your problems to disappear, imagine chipping away at them as you eat blueberries one by one.

For even more complex and potent food magic, try these recipes—no magic crab needed.

IF YOU WANT ▸ to chill out
MAKE ▸ warm milk with honey

Jaya's dad made this for her as a kid when she couldn't sleep. To this day it has a calming effect. (Also, honey is a natural antiseptic. Dab it on cuts or zits for healing power.)

Fill a mug with your favorite kind of milk, and then pour it into a small saucepan. Add a tablespoon of honey, and place it over low heat, stirring often so the honey dissolves. When it reaches a simmer, remove from heat and pour the milk back into the mug. Next, sit wherever you plan to drink your beverage, and hold the mug in both hands, feeling the warmth begin to radiate up your arms. Look into the milk, and recite the following:

Let my mind be calm
My nerves quiet
Muscles smooth as silk

Let my body fill up
With warmth and peace
From this honey and milk

IF YOU WANT ▸ to nurture a friendship
MAKE ▸ hot milk chocolate

Milk chocolate has nurturing power, especially when it comes to friendship. Also, it's *milk chocolate*, so we probably don't have to sell you on it (unless you're allergic, in which case, please don't make yourself sick for the sake of a spell). You can share milk chocolate with a friend in lots of ways, like buying a bar and eating it together. However, hot chocolate has the potential to enhance the bonding, especially if the weather is cold and warm blankets are involved.

First, grate a bar of milk chocolate until you have about 2 ounces (about ½ cup) of grated chocolate. (You can add some dark chocolate if you like, but for maxiumum potency use mostly milk.) Next, warm 2 cups of milk in a small saucepan (aka your cauldron) over medium heat.

When the milk reaches a simmer, reduce the heat to low, add 1 teaspoon of brown sugar, and stir until it dissolves.

Now sprinkle the grated chocolate into the milk mixture and stir while visualizing yourself and your friend: a particularly meaningful conversation you've had, a fond memory of a fun shared experience, or just all the things you like about the person. If you're making the hot chocolate together, say these things out loud!

When the chocolate is dissolved, add a pinch of salt, both for spiritual cleansing and because it strengthens the chocolate flavor. As you add the salt, speak or think this incantation:

Friends for now
Friends forever
May the elements tie us together

IF YOU WANT ▶ to attract a lover
MAKE ▶ baked apples with cinnamon

You know what's warm, comforting, and a little tingly and spicy? Cinnamon. You know what else fits that description? The feeling of having a new crush. Maybe that's why the spice is associated with fire and the sun and is used often in spells to draw love. Apples, too, are used for love, partially because of their connotation as the sexy "forbidden fruit." (The actual forbidden fruit of the Bible was probably closer to a pomegranate, but those don't work as well with cinnamon.)

This spell works especially well if you have access to an open fire, such as in a fireplace or at a backyard bonfire gathering of your coven. If not, you can make it in the oven (though there's less space for wild dancing in your kitchen).

In a small bowl, combine ¼ teaspoon of cinnamon and 1 tablespoon of brown sugar. Core an apple (a sturdy, tart one works best, like Granny Smith or Fuji) and fill the core with the cinnamon mixture. Wrap the apple in tinfoil, and place it in the embers of a fire to cook for about 7 minutes. If you don't have an open fire, preheat an oven to 350°F, place the stuffed apple in an ovenproof dish, and bake for 15 minutes.

As the apple cooks, stare into the embers (or close your eyes if you're baking in an oven) and picture your crush. Envision that the warmth currently radiating onto you is radiating onto them, filling them with the fire you feel within and making them aware that it's coming from you. Carefully remove the apple from the fire or oven and let it cool for around 3 minutes, or until cool enough to handle.

Sit cross-legged on the ground (or floor) and hold the apple with both hands. Eat it as messily as you can. Grunt and hum as you chew, and let the sugar and cinnamon dribble down your hands. Let yourself feel wild and magnetic. And the next time you see your crush, remember just how carnal you were in this moment.

IF YOU WANT ▶ boundless energy
MAKE ▶ banana ice cream

With the power of electricity and sharp knives, you can transform fruit into a one-ingredient soft serve ice cream. Bananas are associated with heroic energy and protection, as are blenders (yes, witches have given power to blenders), so make this to motivate yourself to achieve greatness.

Slice 2 bananas, place them in a zip-top freezer bag, and seal the bag. Freeze until bananas are very firm (probably overnight). In a food processor or blender, blend the frozen banana slices for 3 to 5 minutes, until the texture resembles soft-serve ice cream.

While plain bananas are delicious, you can further enhance the power of this dessert with flavorings: chopped cherries for love, honey for happiness, or coconut for mental flexibility.

IF YOU WANT ▶ beauty
MAKE ▶ guacamole

The avocado is a very femme fruit, associated with Venus and the element of water, both of which make it useful in spells pertaining to love and beauty. It has nonmagical beautifying qualities, too; its high fat content makes for a great natural face or hair mask. But by enchanting the fruit and ingesting it, you can fill yourself up with that beautifying power to make you feel as pretty and charming as you already are.

Start by enchanting the avocado. Slice it in half while saying what you want to happen, such as "I want to feel radiant" or "I want others to notice how beautiful I know I am." Remove and reserve the pit, then slice the avocado flesh in the skin and spoon the flesh from the skin into a bowl. Add half of a freshly chopped tomato (seeds and juices removed), 1 minced serrano chili, 2 tablespoons minced red onion, 1 tablespoon fresh lime juice, 1 tablespoon chopped cilantro, and salt and pepper to taste. Mix with a fork while repeating your enchantment, and eat with whatever chips make you feel like a babe. When you've finished the guac, wash and dry the pit and carry it with you for a week to keep the gorgeous vibes going.

If all this symbolism and emotion isn't quite your style, you can simply think of cooking as a form of therapeutic creation. You start with nothing and, by solving one problem at a time, wind up with something beautiful, or delicious, or maybe just edible. No matter how it turns out, you've brought something new into the world.

Magical Exercise

HOW TO BECOME ONE FIT WITCH

~~~

Exercise can—and should—be a way of taking care of yourself: physical activity not only gets your body strong and limber, but also helps your brain combat depression and anxiety. But it might not feel that way if your exercise routine consists solely of joyless hours spent trudging on the treadmill. Too often, we treat exercise like a boring, slightly bitter-tasting medicine that's supposed to make us feel better afterward.

A spoonful of sugar may help actual medicine go down, but it's not the greatest incentive for exercise. What if instead you bribed yourself with a spoonful of *swords*?

Okay, you are not literally going to *swallow* swords. (That's a whole other thing.) But you can learn how to brandish them. If you're bored with your everyday workout, consider picking up an unconventional physical activity—especially one that teaches you some unruly woman skills. Like alchemy, the exertion and the new skill training combine to make your exercise routine enjoyable. Here are a few ideas (appropriate for a few different levels of physical ability) for workouts that will not only energize your body and mind but also leave you with new witchy skills.

Swordplay: If you dream of being not only a sorceress but a magic-wielding warrior, look for classes in fencing, kendo, or even longsword (google "historical European martial arts" plus your city or town). Be prepared: you're in for some heavy-duty bruising once you start to spar. But if you're the kind of person who likes hitting other people with swords, you'll probably love it. (Jess is the kind of person who likes hitting other people with swords and is confident about this point.)

Dance: Any kind of dance will help you feel graceful and at home in your body—not to mention more confident at midnight coven boogies in the moonlit woods. Jess does belly dance, which is great for proprioception and bodily control because you learn to isolate different muscle groups; Jaya does pole dance, which increases strength and flexibility, as well as sexiness. But maybe you want to do flamenco, hip-hop, or salsa—lots of dance styles can increase power and grace, and many are appropriate for a range of skill levels and physical capabilities.

Contact juggling: If you've seen David Bowie in *Labyrinth* rolling a crystal ball between his hands in a way that's almost as magical and mesmerizing as his tight pants, you're familiar with contact juggling. It's the sport of choice for crystal gazers and goblin kings alike. (Also, you can juggle and jog, which is known as "joggling." Not making that up.)

Aerials: You're a witch, so why not learn to fly? Aerials—tricks and artistry on equipment like trapeze and hanging silks—is a physically demanding pursuit, like a cross between ballet and rock climbing. But you don't have to be a stunning athlete to try it—you just need a lot of determination. Jess has a friend who made a New Year's resolution to be able to do one single pull-up, and by the end of the year she had started taking an aerials class. Two years later, she was performing. (And yeah, she could do a pull-up, but more importantly she could *hold herself in the air on a trapeze*.)

Quidditch: Until we can fly around on broomsticks, the next best thing may be a sport in which people run around with broomsticks between their legs, pretending to fly. Quidditch, of course, comes from the world of Harry Potter, where it involves flying and magic—but there are real-world leagues too, which rely on the magic of imagination and endorphins. (And real athletic prowess—the U.S. Quidditch website describes the sport as a combination of rugby, dodgeball, and tag.) Playing quidditch may not teach you to ride a broomstick, but it offers ample training in another important witch skill: not giving a shit if other people think you look ridiculous. Check out www.usquidditch.org to find a team near you.

Shuffleboard: Nowadays, we may think of shuffleboard as a sport reserved for grandpas, but it has a rebellious, witchy history (plus it offers a pretty good shoulder workout). According to one of her descendants, Bridget Bishop, who was accused of witchcraft in Salem, Massachusetts, was an outspoken woman who spent a lot of time hanging out with sailors in her tavern. As if that weren't bad enough, she had the audacity "to entertain people in her house at unseasonable hours in the night to keep drinking and playing at shuffleboard, whereby discord did arise in other families, and young people were in danger to be corrupted," according to Paul Boyer and Stephen Nissenbaum in *Salem Possessed*.

WITCH CALISTHENICS

1.
Stirring the cauldron
While standing, hold your arms straight out to your sides and rotate your hands in small circles, first forward and then backward.

2.
Raising the dead
Lie on your back with knees bent and use your core muscles to lift your shoulders off the floor. Keep your feet flat on the ground and your eyes on the ceiling. Repeat.

3.
Light as a feather, stiff as a board
Lie on your stomach. Keeping your body in a straight line, support yourself on your hands and toes. Your hands should be directly under your shoulders.

4.
The broomstick
Stand with feet parallel and shoulder width apart. Bend your knees as close to 90 degrees as possible, pushing your hands out in front of you and your butt in the opposite direction. Repeat.

5.
The flying monkey
Stand with feet 4 to 5 feet apart, and rotate one foot out. Turn your torso to face that side, and bend the front knee to a 90-degree angle. Don't let your knee go past your foot. Repeat on both sides.

6.
Possession
Lie facedown on the ground, then lift your shoulders, arms, and legs as far as you can. Lower and repeat.

A RITUAL FOR

A Relaxing
Netflix Binge

Witches are allowed to relax, and watching endless episodes of TV is a fine way to do it. Use this ritual to help cast off your guilt and give yourself permission to go deep.

WHAT YOU'LL NEED:

The biggest blanket you can find

Your favorite snack

Your favorite streaming service, ready to watch

Good television and movies are a conduit to other worlds, experiences, and lives: a fictional little boy with superpowers, or a lonely teenage girl, or a rich family a thousand miles away. Immersing yourself in their universe via Netflix binge can transport you not only mentally, but also emotionally. There is also catharsis in watching bad television, which can provide the healing magic of putting yourself not just elsewhere, but nowhere. Because although spells and witchcraft may be all about stimulating the brain, sometimes you just want your brain to turn off.

The trick, however, is to watch without judgment. Society puts so much pressure on us to be constantly productive—even our time to ourselves is supposed to be mentally or physically stimulating. A ritual is the perfect way to create the accepting space needed for this ultimate disappearing act.

Sit cross-legged and throw the blanket over your head, so your whole body is completely covered. Close your eyes, and envision the blanket slowly turning into a warm, golden ball of light. Then begin to hum, imagining all your stress, guilt, or other concerns emanating from your body and into the golden ball, where they break apart and disappear.

As the stress leaves your body, envision the golden light entering, filling you up and making every cell radiate. Take stock of your emotions: Would a sad movie make you feel sadder, or do you want to revel in those feelings? Do you want the comfort of watching a show you've seen a dozen times, or are you ready to try something new?

When you feel like you have a good sense of what you want to watch, emerge from the blanket, and take a bite of your snack. You are now ready to start watching.

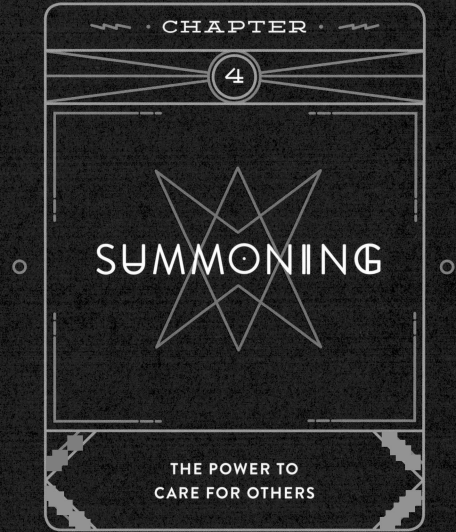

SUMMONING

THE POWER TO
CARE FOR OTHERS

We think of the witch as a solitary creature. She lives alone on the edge of town in a ragged house surrounded by weeds, emerging only at night, happily separated from other living beings (save maybe a cat or a newt). But nothing could be further from the truth: witches love to travel in packs, or, as we call them, covens.

Finding a group of like-minded people to share your feelings, passions, and powers with is not something that happens all of a sudden. There's not a store where you can just pick up a set of friends (though there are apps, which is sort of the same). Cultivating a strong social circle is an active process. Your coven isn't just the group of people who happen to show up in the same places as you do, but the people you've chosen to devote part of your heart and mind (and schedule) to. You will not always agree with them. You may not always understand the decisions they make. They will not always make you happy (though if they're making you miserable, you may want to reevaluate). But in the end, they are the people you show up for.

Covens aren't necessarily intuitive, either. Many people like to have a "best friend," but there's more to your coven than your favorite, closest pal. The people you choose to join you will have different purposes at different times. Sometimes your energies will be synced with one person more than others, and sometimes others won't be as connected to one another as they are to you. But your coven is your team. Together, you're greater than any one—or even any two—of you alone.

In this chapter, we'll talk about seeking out and evaluating potential friends, navigating jealousy and competitiveness, healing conflicts, and joining forces with the weird sisters who recognize your powers. Maintaining a coven requires selflessness, compromise, and deep empathy. But when done right, all of that energy is reciprocal and comes back many times over. If these are the people you show up for, they are also the people who will show up for you, at your best and at your worst, however you grow and change. No matter what happens, they will be there for you, ready to strip and dance naked in the woods.

How to Build a Coven

~~~

Good coven-building relies on one of the core pillars of many witchcraft practices: the rule of threes, also known as the threefold law or the law of return. Basically, whatever energy you put into the world, you will receive in return three times stronger. This rule is good to keep in mind no matter what you're doing, but especially when making friends.

Everyone understands that if you're a thoughtful, caring person you tend to attract thoughtful, caring people, and if you're mean and vindictive, it'll eventually come around to bite you in the ass. But the rule of threes adds an urgency to that common knowledge. When building a coven, the rule of threes applies not just to energy, but actual people. If you lie about who you are and don't treat the people in your life well, you may soon find yourself surrounded by people treating you three times worse than you ever treated anyone—or worse, surrounded by no one at all.

▶ ▶ ▶ Start with your present coven.

Because you're old enough to read a book independently, you've likely lived long enough to pick up a few friends. If these friends have been close and cool and loyal from day one, and you can share your deepest feelings and fears with them, then fantastic. Keep doing what you're doing.

However, maybe you're not comfortable with the friends you have right now. That happened to Jaya in middle school. Her group of friends *said* they loved her but put her down for her appearance, weight, interests, and basically anything else they could pick on. She was afraid to tell them she was hurt, felt pressured to do what they told her, and never really felt like they would be there for her in a crisis. But she ignored those feelings, because these were her friends. They had been around for years, and starting over seemed scary. Salvation came in the form of a new school, summer camp, and a group of people who accepted Jaya for her complete, weird self. But it also came as Jaya began to realize what made her *her*. This included surface stuff like music tastes and fashion choices, but also her particular way of looking at the world.

In terms of the rule of three, it's not just good energy but your own unique energy that brings back good returns, in the form of others who truly understand you. If you're getting back nothing but negative vibes, you may be wasting your aura on the wrong crowd. Being yourself isn't just a statement or a boost for your self-esteem, it's literally attractive—it brings people toward you.

▶ ▶ ▶ Find where they're hiding.

Because friendships often begin with shared interests, spend time in places and doing activities you enjoy. You could meet a potential new coven-mate at a play or at a concert, on a sports team or in a hiking club, or at a Magic: The Gathering competition at your local comic book store. Surface interests often correlate with deeper similarities.

If you're not the club-joining type, identify someone in your life who seems cool that you want to get to know better. All good relationships balance self-acceptance and growth, after all. A truly powerful bond will leave you feeling as comfortable as possible with yourself (because no one feels comfortable with themselves 100 percent of the time), but also open to change. Good friends won't ask you to apologize for the things you love and will lead you to new things you don't know you love yet.

▶ ▶ ▶ Practice patience.

Assembling a coven doesn't happen overnight. You won't show up on the first day of volleyball practice and walk away with a new best friend for life. In fact, one of the best pieces of advice Jaya was given when headed off to college was *not* to try to make friends, which seems counterintuitive. The logic went that, especially in a dorm-room setting, making fast friends is easy (and fast friends are okay!), but if you can slowly get to know people, quality connections will reveal themselves. (It totally worked.) Divining who is truly coven-worthy takes time. If hanging out with someone leaves you feeling powered up, excited, or relaxed, that's a strong sign that this person is compatible. If afterward you're drained, anxious, or even bored, they might be sapping you of strength instead.

▸▸▸ Be bold.

Asking someone to get closer to you can be scary, like asking someone on a date. But if you have the courage to take that risk, your effort will be returned to you threefold. The easiest way to bridge the gap is to move forward. Ask them to hang out, invite them places you're going, get their number and start texting them. Pay attention to how they react to your advances; tune in very carefully to their energy and use it to bolster your own feelings of friendship and connection. Even if the friendship doesn't become super-close super-fast, you'll have increased your powers of self-confidence simply by putting them into practice.

▸▸▸ Don't curse your chances.

If you've been less than perfect in your past relationships—whether you were your high school's mean girl or a total outcast—you're not doomed to be lonely forever. You can still find a stronger, more nurturing community whenever you're ready to seek it out. Tap deep into your psyche and become especially aware of your actions. How are you treating people? Are you being there for them like you want them to be there for you? If what you're doing came back to you threefold, how would you feel?

Most importantly, you must trust in your magic. Insecurity over making friends often stems from fear that you have nothing to offer, that no one would want to join your coven. But people are out there who match your magic, and they will not only value it but be energized by it. Sharing and affirming the essence of who you are may take time and it may take work, but it is always worth it.

WITCH HISTORY

THE WOMEN'S INTERNATIONAL
TERRORIST CONSPIRACY
FROM HELL

ON HALLOWEEN MORNING, 1968, thirteen women dressed as witches marched toward the New York Stock Exchange—dancing, singing, and carrying a papier-mâché pig's head on a platter. After telling security that they had an appointment with "the Boss, Satan," the women made their way to the trading floor, where they hexed the entire enterprise. The market closed that day 1.5 points down and dropped a further five points the next day.

This group of activists, known as the Women's International Terrorist Conspiracy from Hell (get it?), was active only for a few years in the late 1960s, but in that time it used magic and mischief to protest capitalism, patriarchal beauty standards, and the institution of marriage. The first W.I.T.C.H. coven was founded by New York City feminists who found local activism too serious and not mischievous enough, and soon sister covens popped up in other cities. These thirteen-member groups would get together to cast hexes on symbols of oppression, ranging from the presidential inauguration to beauty pageants to the Chicago Transit Authority after a fare hike.

Their approach was certainly radical at the time, but in many ways, the tactics of W.I.T.C.H. seem almost embarrassingly retro now. The group's manifesto talks about "gypsies," a term now understood to be a racist slur against the Romani people. It attacked women for participating in the sexist system of marriage—the New York coven infiltrated a bridal show held in Madison Square Garden, chanting "Here come the slaves, off to their graves" and papering the city with stickers saying "Confront the Whore-Makers at the Bridal Fair"—although original member Robin Morgan wrote in her 1977 book *Going Too Far: The Personal Chronicle of a Feminist*, "We thought it would be clear that this time we were blaming the *men* who forced women into the institution of marriage, not pillorying the *women*. We might have realized that brides-to-be don't like being called whores." (Of course, even using "whore" as an insult is retro; many feminists today support sex workers, and don't call them names either.)

Still, in other ways W.I.T.C.H. was astonishingly modern. "If you are a woman and dare to look within yourself, you are a Witch. You make your own rules. You are both free and beautiful. You can be invisible or evident in how you choose to make your witch-self known," read the group's manifesto. "Whatever is repressive, solely male-oriented, greedy, puritanical, authoritarian—those are your targets. . . . Your power comes from your own self as a woman, and it is activated by working together with your sisters." We can't argue with that—that's the kind of witchcraft this book is all about.

A TAROT RITUAL TO

Attract Friendship

WHAT YOU'LL NEED:

Like a love spell, this ritual will not blindly bind someone to you, but make you the most attractive version of yourself. You'll use the symbolism of the tarot to channel your energy into your future relationships.

A deck of tarot cards (find them in bookstores, specialty shops, or online)

A fancy goblet (or cup) of water

Remove the Three of Cups and the Sun from the tarot deck. The Sun, when upright, represents optimism, fulfillment, and the happiness that comes from being one's truest self. It symbolizes who you are in your friendship journey. The Three of Cups represents friendship, community, and the celebration of those things. It symbolizes where you want to wind up in your journey.

Sitting on the floor, make a triangle with the cards and your body, with the Sun to your upper left and the Three of Cups to your upper right. Place the goblet of water in the middle of the triangle. Close your eyes, and picture a strand of gold thread connecting you to the Sun, charging the card with all the attributes you'll bring to any new friendship. Then picture that thread extending from the Sun to the Three of Cups, taking your energy out into the community. Finally, join the thread from the Three of Cups back to you, so that the positive energy you put into the Sun is now flowing back to you through friendship.

Sit for as long as you need to more clearly envision your future, in which you're opening yourself up to the world and receiving love and trust in return. When you're done, pick up the goblet and drink the water. Carry the two cards with you until you start making connections.

The Transformative Power of Vulnerability

〜〜〜

Meeting new people, making overtures, and building familiarity take work, and once you've forged a friendship, you may be tempted to treat it like a fragile treasure. You get anxious about putting any kind of pressure on the relationship—after all, if it breaks, you have to start all over again. But you can't have a whole, true, nourishing friendship if you're frightened to ask for anything or show your darker side. Luckily, witches don't shy away from demons—they consort with them, not only bravely but merrily. Members of a strong, supportive coven will help you figure out how to recognize your demons, resist their worst influences, and even dance alongside them. At the very least, your coven should be willing to invite your demons to happy hour. But there's no way to confront these agents of darkness without being open, honest, and vulnerable.

Not all decent friendships delve into dark territory. But being able to admit to being scared, or sad, or uncertain, or hurt, or haunted by the past can add a special dimension to a friendship (and a romantic relationship; more on that in the next chapter).

So how do you start being vulnerable? Here are some ideas.

▶ ▶ ▶ Create space to summon demons without fear.

At the heart of vulnerability is openness: a willingness to reveal yourself, but also to accept others. But even more important than sharing is listening. Don't overwhelm your friends by dumping problems on them; show yourself to be a compassionate ear, a careful thinker, an active participant in cultivating a judgment-free environment. Think back to the rule of threes: the more openness you give to others, the more you'll receive when it's your turn to share.

▶▶▶ Join in the dance.
Instead of hiding what you're going through, bring your demon to the party and see how that feels. Does being open about a personal struggle overwhelm your group and suck all the air out of the room? Or can all of you look the demon in the eye and help each other not to flinch? Challenge yourself to acknowledge negative thoughts and feelings instead of merely sweeping them under the rug.

▶▶▶ Find your demons' true names.
This part of vulnerability is less about figuring out how to formally address your demons and more about exploring their nature. If you want to read about some demons with fancy Latinate names that, quite frankly, we made up, check out page 160—but learning to name your demons is more about recognizing their true nature. Vulnerability doesn't mean just blurting out complaints—"I'm sad," "I'm lonely," "what you said made me angry," "my knee hurts." It means exploring and sharing the reasons behind your anger, sadness, and pain. When that's hard to do alone, an insightful friend should be able to help. Be sincere, flexible, and willing to entertain multiple causes of (and solutions to) your problems. Opening up about a problem but then sneering at every proposed solution is not vulnerability—that's just bitching.

▶▶▶ Resist the allure of wallowing (and mistreatment).
Sometimes sharing your darkest, ugliest struggles can rebound in unfortunate ways: your friend might enable further toxic thinking instead of helping you banish it, or she might simply be careless with your secrets. (If you need to establish protection around yourself, try the spells on pages 101 and 126.) Don't kick yourself too hard. The process of opening up, regardless of the outcome, will help you learn to look your demons in the face and, eventually, dance with them on your own.

Deepen Friendship

Good friends create happy memories but also understand your sadness and secrets without judgment. This ritual celebrates all the many aspects at the heart of friendship.

WHAT YOU'LL NEED:

A collection of objects

A cigar box or other small container

This ritual requires prep work by both you and your friend. Before you meet, meditate on difficult memories, personal traumas, anxieties, perceived flaws, and secrets you want her to understand. (We're calling your friend "her," but these friendship spells work with friends of all genders.) Then find or make a small token to represent each of these experiences or qualities: create small artworks, or find inexpensive objects to represent your secrets (for example, a plastic ring could symbolize your worry about finding a life partner, a playing card could represent fear that your success is due to luck instead of skill, or a dry leaf could indicate anxiety about aging). Collect six to eight of these and put them in the box. Have your friend do the same.

Meet your friend in a quiet, comfortable, familiar place with your boxes. Explain to her what each item in the box represents, then have her do the same for her items. Then present your box to her, saying:

I give you my sadness, not as a burden but as a gift.

When your friend accepts the box, she should say:

I accept your sadness, not to cure but to protect.

Then repeat the exchange with your friend's box of secrets.

For the following week, contemplate the items in your friend's collection. Think about happy memories you've shared or future plans. Create a new association for each item she's given you: for example, the plastic ring could be a reminder of a fun shopping trip at a flea market, the playing card could symbolize your shared love for *Alice in Wonderland,* and the dry leaf could represent your upcoming hiking adventure.

When a week has passed, meet your friend again in the same place. Tell her the new meanings you've devised for her objects. Then have her do the same for your objects.

Present your friend's box of secrets, now a box of happy thoughts, back to her, saying:

*I give you what we share together, though I still protect
your sadness in my heart.*

When your friend accepts the box, she should say:

*I accept this as a treasure, though our bonds are both light
and dark.*

Repeat the exchange with the other box. Keep your original box, which now contains both your shared vulnerabilities and happiness, in a safe place in your home.

WHICH PET SHOULD BE YOUR FAMILIAR?

Cat
Pros: Low-maintenance, fuzzy, doesn't give a shit about anyone's opinions
Cons: Sharp, weird, doesn't give a shit about your opinions

Dog
Pros: Unconditional love, can learn tricks, extreme power over emotions
Cons: Sorta dumb, totally filthy, will absolutely betray you to your enemies

Guinea Pig
Pros: Squeaks adorably, tolerates costumes, can easily hide while spying on people for you
Cons: No good for sawdust allergies, not good pack animals, soulless eyes

Cockatiel
Pros: Tiny dinosaur, can fly, totally punk rock
Cons: Tiny dinosaur, can be a jerk, difficult to walk

Snake
Pros: Smells with its tongue and that's badass, scales, as venomous as my heart
Cons: Walk with its abs and that's weird, not all are venomous, phallic

Manatee
Pros: Huggable, often mistaken for mermaids, body positive
Cons: Confined to the water, illegal to touch in Florida (but don't touch anything in any state without its consent)

Healing Friends for Fun and Profit

HOW TO CHANNEL YOUR INNER WISE WOMAN

～

Emotional work—like listening, thinking, and advising—is *work*, though often we think of it as "just part of friendship" or "just something women like to do." But donating comfort and solace to a friend is a labor of love, just like knitting a sweater or making a pie. The healers and wise women who were later called witches recognized the value of this effort; their life's mission was to look after the physical and emotional health of their community, after all. But although they might have been able to cure a broken heart with a potion, or devise a ritual to ease someone's nerves, or concoct a salve for sadness, they also expected fair compensation.

When a friend comes to you with a problem, you can imagine yourself as the village wise woman or healing crone: A young woman of the community has approached you with her problem—heartbreak, say. She has braved difficulties traveling to your hut, which is far from the village, maybe even in a perilous place, and she feels ashamed of anyone knowing that she's there or why. But she knows she's hurting and will take some risks to find help. She has brought payment, though not necessarily money; she knows she doesn't owe you something just because she's in need.

How would the village witch handle such a request?

▶ ▶ ▶ Affirm the difficulty of seeking help.

As we've seen earlier in the chapter, admitting to another person that you're in pain is often a tremendous act of will, and the path to relief isn't always straightforward. Don't judge your friend for needing your healing, and don't expect her to be able to tell you exactly what she needs. Helping her figure that out is part of the service you can provide.

▶ ▶ ▶ Recognize the healing value you possess.

Often when someone is in pain, our first instinct is to say something like "I wish there were something I could do." That may be good-hearted, but it's also dismissive, because there *is* something you can do: listen, keep her company, help her think or plan or laugh or grieve.

▶ ▶ ▶ Use the magic words.

"Do you want advice, or do you want to vent?" "Would it help to talk more about what happened?" "What do you plan to do next?" "Do you need someone to go with you?"

MODERN CURES FOR EMOTIONAL ILLS

Potions and tinctures: Let your friend tell you her troubles over tea, cocoa, or cocktails. You're buying.

A familiar: Invite a sad friend to play with your pets, or act as a familiar yourself by accompanying her to do an emotionally difficult task.

Curses and laughter spells: Depending on your friend's situation, she may be aided by you expressing your anger alongside her or by you helping her to laugh and forget her troubles. If you're not sure which, ask.

Objects of power: Thoughtful gifts and care packages sent to a distant friend are a way to help from afar.

Advice: But not scolding or lectures! If you're not sure whether advice is welcome, you can always ask first.

▶ ▶ ▶ Consider your price.

You don't owe anyone free emotional labor—but you can offer the people you love a special deal. Before offering to help, consider how much it requires from you (Will you need to accompany this person somewhere? Make a difficult phone call for them? Help them draft a tricky letter?) and how much you're likely to get in repayment (gratitude, seeing them happy, similar help from them in the future). If your assistance is grossly out of proportion with the likely payback, that's a good way to breed exhaustion and resentment. So offer all you reasonably can and no more.

Don't think of yourself as wise enough to be the village wise woman? Don't let that stop you. If a friend comes to you for help, she probably considers you a healer, even if you don't identify as an expert in emotional health. (After all, the village wise women were hardly licensed therapists.) The important thing is to put in the effort—and to recognize that helping does take effort, that it's a kind and difficult thing you can do for a friend.

Establishing Boundaries

In this ritual, a magic protective circle symbolizes the boundaries that keep you safe within your friendship.

WHAT YOU'LL NEED:

At least 10 index cards

A pen

Chalk or salt

A small cup of water, if you're using chalk

2 folders or envelopes

Magic depends on harmony and balance, and a harmonious friendship requires balance between vulnerability and boundaries. Boundaries protect you in relationships that become emotionally unsafe, carry obligations, or take up more time and energy than you can spare. As you get closer with a friend, you will likely find that your boundaries shift.

The protective circle is a simple piece of magic popular among practicing witches and is, of course, a boundary. Whether you encounter malign forces or just need an area to concentrate and feel safe, the protective circle creates an energy space that can't be broached—even by you, until you've symbolically opened a doorway. You can return to this ritual again and again as your relationship develops.

Perform this ritual in a room where the floor is easy to clean (concrete, tile, or linoleum are all good surfaces.) On each index card, write or draw one thing that a friend might ask of you, either with her or on your own. Come up with at least 10 asks, trying for a mix of ones that push your boundaries and others that don't. Some ideas for friendship activities that usually don't push boundaries: sharing triumphs and joys, going to a movie together, celebrating a birthday, discussing favorite books. Some ideas for friendship activities that not everyone wants to do with every friend: talking on the phone, discussing your sex lives, discussing your diets, expressing sadness or trauma, texting frequently, doing personal grooming (like waxing) appointments together. You can focus on a particular friend, tailoring your choices to your friendship, or practice the ritual for general boundary-setting, sticking to generic requests and friend favors.

With the chalk, or the salt, make a circle on the ground at least three feet in diameter. As you draw, say these words:

What I invite into my heart, let me invite it into this circle.
What I remove from this circle, let me protect my heart against it.

Stand or sit in the center of the circle. Look at each index card one at a time, picturing yourself doing the activity with another person (or the particular friend, if your ritual is specific to one person). Notice how you feel. If contemplating the card makes you feel joyful, excited, or another positive emotion, place it on the ground inside the circle. Otherwise, place it outside the circle.

When you have contemplated all the cards, open a door in your friendship circle by washing away some of the chalk with the water or by brushing away some of the salt. As you open the door, say these words:

Let my heart remain open even as I protect myself.
Let me protect myself even as my heart remains open.

You may now leave the circle. Collect the two piles of cards and store them in separate folders or envelopes. You can revisit them when you need to remind yourself of your boundaries, and you can repeat the ritual as many times as you want.

WITCH HISTORY
WHY WITCHES DANCE
NAKED IN THE WOODS

SCANDALOUS RUMORS OF WOMEN cavorting with each other in the dark have long accompanied accusations of witchcraft. Although nakedness wasn't considered inherently sinful in the Middle Ages—it also symbolized innocence or youth—it was regarded as outside the norm, enough to be plausible evidence of consort with the devil. Early illustrations and texts depict witches anointing their naked bodies in order to fly. The *Malleus Maleficarum* said witches "have often been seen lying on their backs in the fields or the woods, naked up to the very navel," appearing to have sex with invisible demons. By the 1800s, European artists realized that "a bunch of naked women dancing madly in the middle of the night" was dynamite subject material for a painting (especially if you wanted to paint, well, a bunch of naked women) and created tableaux where the witches in question look less like withered, shameful crones and more like voluptuous, rosy-faced babes (albeit babes flying around with fire-eyed bat-demons). Other depictions of the witches' Sabbat include in-the-buff dancing, sex, and cannibalism, each act as sinful as the next.

But for witches, ritual nudity isn't about sex—it's about freedom. The 1899 book *Aradia, or The Gospel of the Witches*, an influential text in the twentieth-century witchcraft movement, explains it this way: "And as the sign that ye are truly free, Ye shall be naked in your rites, both men and women also." The practice of naked rites—or "going skyclad"—was later embraced by Gerald Gardner, one of the founders of Wicca.

Modern witches practice ritual nudity to get as close as possible to the earth and spirits. It's also a way to signify faith: "For skyclad covens, 'skin is the livery of the Goddess;' it is *their* Sunday or Sabbath best," according to *A Witches' Bible*. Also, like showing up to church or synogogue (no matter what you're wearing), naked group dancing is about community. Praying from home is fine, but putting on (or taking off) a nice dress and meeting up with your peers gives your spiritual practice extra resonance.

Worshipping the Moon
with Shine Theory

~~~

In a 2013 *New York* magazine article, writer Ann Friedman coined the term "shine theory": the idea that when remarkable women surround themselves with other remarkable women, we make each other shine more brightly. The idea seems almost counterintuitive: we are taught to be wary of other women *out*shining us, and this anxiety fuels everything from slam books to corporate backstabbing to hideous bridesmaid dresses with giant bows on the butt. But it's rooted in an idea of false scarcity, a *Highlander*-style conviction that for one woman to succeed, all others must fail.

Helping one another shine is important to witches, who have long found the moon—associated with spirituality, magic, and feminine power—symbolically significant for similar reasons: it's reflective, not incandescent, but it's no less beautiful or important for relying on borrowed light. It may not be a gigantic nuclear furnace, but nobody would say that the moon doesn't shine—and on bright moonlit nights, it allows water to shine, too, and grass, and windows, and trees. If there's snow on the ground, the shine can be bright enough to read by.

If you believe that you have to fight other women for the hottest guy, the "token woman" spot on the board, or the queen bee social role, you are turning away from the shine. A man who encourages you to insult or betray other women is hardly a prize. A company that refuses to hire more than one woman is bound to be toxic. The social capital of a queen bee pales in comparison to an entire coven of bright, creative, synergistic, supportive pals.

Embracing the light in other women expands options for everyone. Shine theory encourages us to realize that there is enough success and happiness and confidence and love to go around—that, in fact, there's more of it when women support each other.

If you are stuck in the habit of competing and comparing, try going outside on a clear night during a full moon for a shine theory ritual. Imagine yourself surrounded by friends, each of you softly glowing in the moonlight. Speak this incantation aloud to each imagined friend in turn, until it feels natural and easy:

I'm so proud of you.
I'm lucky to know you.
I'm lucky I get to be your friend.

You may also want to bring a talisman to charge with the feeling of being bathed in reflected light, or a jar or vial in which to collect some of the moonlight and help keep the feeling going.

Ditch Friend Envy

WHAT YOU'LL NEED:

This spell will help you expel jealous thoughts from your mind while focusing your energies on the positive.

2 pieces of paper, one larger than the other

A pen or pencil

Light-blue and yellow crayons or colored pencils

Despite our best intentions to be bright shining moons for each other, even the most generous people sometimes succumb to friend envy. Maybe your friend is doing better in school or in her career than you feel you are. Maybe she's dating someone you liked first, or dating while you're single. Maybe her hair looked amazing on a day when you woke up feeling bad about yourself. (How dare she.) Addressing this (totally normal) jealousy will help both of you get your glow back.

On the small piece of paper, write down what your friend has that you want. Be as specific as possible. Instead of just writing "a boy-friend," for example, dig a little deeper—why do you envy her relation-ship? Because you want to feel loved and appreciated? Because you want to know that someone has your back? Because you just want to borrow a big comfy sweatshirt?

On the larger piece of paper, list everything you have that brings joy to your life. Be as broad or as specific as you want—"the ability to appreciate beauty" is just as good as "that endearing little hair below my belly button."

Envision two energy bubbles of equal size, a green one containing envy and a pink one containing joy. Read the list on the larger piece of paper out loud three times. As you speak each item, picture the green bubble shrinking and the pink bubble expanding and crowding it out.

Fold the small piece of paper into as tiny a square as you can make and place it inside the larger one. Fold the larger piece of paper into a square around it. Then use the crayons to decorate this little feelings packet (light blue for tranquility and understanding; yellow for breaking down mental blocks). Scribble nonsense doodles, spell out words, sketch a detailed image—whatever your feelings inspire. As you draw, imagine your bitterness draining from you with every stroke, leaving only the belief that you—and your friend—deserve good things. Close your eyes, take a few deep breaths, and thank yourself for taking the time to care for yourself. Keep the package in a safe place until your envious feelings dissipate.

Let Go of a Friendship

WHAT YOU'LL NEED:

A pen or pencil

1 chess piece that you feel represents you

1 chess piece that you feel represents the other person

Based on a spell from A Witches' Bible *designed to bring two people closer together, this spell encourages two people to drift apart peacefully.*

Friendship feels precious. Sure, humans make connections every day, but bonding with a person who gets you, who accepts you for your weird or silly or sour self, is some of the strongest magic out there. So it's natural to feel wistful when a friendship wanes. Maybe one or both of you did something unforgivable to the other. Maybe you've grown apart, or your interests and values have changed. Or maybe neither of you has been making an effort and, when you think about it, you realize neither of you minds.

After a romantic breakup, we have a cultural script to follow. We call friends, we mope, we eat ice cream and slowly look for love again. But there is no script for how to react to a friend breakup. Sometimes it makes sense to talk about these changes with your friend, so you can accept what's happening and maybe salvage part of the friendship. But other times, ghosting might make the most sense. We can't tell you what will work for your circumstance. We just know that, whatever it is, a ritual to bid farewell to that relationship never hurts.

With the pen, scratch or write each of your names on the bottom of the respective chess pieces and place them next to each other on the center of a shelf. While placing one hand on each piece, close your eyes and recite the following three times:

It is time to say goodbye
We will each move forward
Thank you for what you have given me

Each day for seven days, recite the incantation and move the pieces a little farther apart, so that after a week they are on opposite ends of the shelf. Then thank each piece for what it has done and put them away.

ENCHANTMENT

THE POWER TO MAKE CHOICES
ABOUT LOVE AND SEX

Unabashed sexuality has always been part of a witch's terrifying power. The witch danced naked. She consorted with lusty demons. She had untrammeled appetites. She took control of her reproduction and helped other women do the same. She "rode around" on a "broomstick," *if you know what we mean.*

Today, women who are secure in, happy about, and in full command of their sexuality are still regarded with suspicion. Our right to control our bodies—from who we want to sleep with to whether we want to get pregnant—is as much a political battleground as it ever was. You're a lot less likely to get burned at the stake, but you're still up against some persistent punishing attitudes about sex. "Slut" is a common insult. Affirmative consent is still somehow a contentious concept. Rape survivors too often are dismissed—even demonized—because of what they were wearing when they were attacked or what kind of social lives they have.

But the power of the witch, the power of the unruly woman who laughs at society's rules, is also the power to transcend all this nonsense by believing unshakably in her right to sexual and romantic expression. We can't tell you how to make everyone else respect your choices, but we can help you respect your own choices so strongly that you don't care what they think.

It can be hard to home in on your own needs and desires with everyone else's expectations whirling around. Whether you love sex or shrug about it or are somewhere in between, at some point you'll either date or be asked why you aren't dating. You'll sleep with those dates or decide you don't want to. You'll meet people who want to sleep with you and decide how you feel about that. You'll be in a relationship or stay single. You'll fall in love or you won't. In all these cases, your inner witch can help get you through.

Conjuring Your Perfect Mate

~~~

Dating often feels less like looking for someone who has exciting qualities and more like systematically ruling out anyone who *doesn't*—especially now that Tinder's a thing. No shirt: swipe left. Dumb name: swipe left. "Loves to laugh": swipe left. Ugh, beard: swipe left.

But in our hypervigilant search for red flags—does he list only male authors on his OkCupid profile? Does she hate dogs? Does he smoke?—we sometimes forget to pay attention to what we do want. It's not enough to know what you won't put up with. You also have to know what might make you happy. Take it from a couple of ladies who goofed up a few times before finding love: "A person, and not wrong for me" is emphatically not the same as "the right person for me." This is where positive visualization can make a huge difference.

By now you know that stating your desires out loud (or at least on paper) is a powerful way to manifest your will in almost every situation. Conjuring up a mate (or date) is no exception. If you find yourself constantly compromising in love, looking for someone *without* many problems instead of someone *with* the ability to fill you with joy, you can benefit from the time-honored technique of conjuring a lovingly detailed imaginary friend.

Jess accidentally discovered this method of attracting romantic connection about a million years ago, when she was 22 and in love with someone emotionally unavailable. Tired of banging her head against that particular wall, she wrote a truly exhaustive description of a hypothetical ideal mate.

He reads everything and remembers the facts and the words he reads
well enough to use them in conversation. He's smarter than I am,
in a field I find interesting. When I initially overreact to something

he says that pushes my buttons, he doesn't immediately counter
my defensiveness and turn it into an actual argument—he has a
way of making me calm down, step back, and be rational without
making me feel like a basket case. He likes doing nice things for
me, and he's willing to ask for help when he needs it, but he doesn't
take advantage of or take for granted the fact that I like doing nice
things for him. He asks my advice on things and then listens. He
gives me advice, but not until I ask. He's devoted to his friends. He
calls his mom. He's incredibly funny, sardonic, great with wordplay,
great deadpan. He knows how to do playful antagonism—he's just
generally playful—but he doesn't make jokes that are actually at my
expense. He's excited about the things he loves, but he's not a particu-
larly driven person and he doesn't get worked up easily. He often
has good ideas for something to do, but sometimes he just wants to
curl up together, and he'll say so.

Then she asked her friends to help give him a name, and she wound up calling him Park (no idea why). Naming her desired partner and enumerating what she wanted from him helped put things in sharp perspective. Every so often she would look at her current Unsuitable Real-Life Fellow— really look at him—and think: "Well, he's no Park." She knew that flings, fun as they were, didn't have to go anywhere because . . . well, they were no Park. And when she finally found the right relationship, the one that felt good everywhere, she looked back at the description she'd written more than a decade before and thought, "Holy shit, this guy is Park."

Jess's friend Kirstin hilariously calls making such a list the "Build-a-Boy Workshop." This method isn't literal magic, of course: detailed contemplation won't conjure your ideal beloved out of thin air. What this exercise can do is remind you that your ideal beloved should be more than just a warm body who isn't too mean to you. And by training your focus on the specific qualities you want, you'll naturally keep your eyes open for their manifestation in the real world, which will, eventually, help you summon that kind of person into your life. Here's how to get started.

▶ ▶ ▶ Go deep.

As you list the positive qualities of your ideal partner, try to go deeper than superficial traits. Rather than all the "favorites" you and your partner have to have in common—favorite band, favorite book, favorite food, etc.—focus on values or emotional traits instead. (In other words, don't be like teen Jaya, whose ideal partner had the same favorite band, but different favorite songs by that band. You know, so they weren't *too* similar. Needless to say, this person never showed up.) Think about what you truly value—not just what you like.

▶ ▶ ▶ Interview your imagination.

Don't know how to divine the meaningful qualities of your ideal partner? Imagine the questions you'd ask at a low-key interview for the position of "my significant other," such as:

+ How do they respond when they disagree with their partner? And when their partner disagrees with them?

+ What kinds of activities do they prioritize?

+ What is their preferred relationship with other friends? With family?

+ What personal life goals are important to them?

+ What does "success" mean for them? What about "happiness"?

▶ ▶ ▶ Know how you want to be loved.

Not everyone shows love the same way. Some people like to have heart-to-heart conversations, give compliments, and otherwise express affection with words. Others like to do favors, buy thoughtful gifts, and perform actions that make life easier for their beloved. When you get involved with someone who expresses love in a different way from you, you may feel smothered or abandoned and pressured to either vilify your partner ("he never buys me presents, what an asshole") or convince yourself to ask for less ("she doesn't express love verbally, so I just have to do without hearing 'I love you,' even though that makes me feel anxious and lonely").

It's important to be open to your partner's ways of expressing love—but it's also okay to need what you need. When you envision your ideal mate, consider what makes you feel loved and cared for. Compliments and verbal affirmation? Cuddling and physical affection? Pampering when you feel down? Sometimes it's embarrassing to admit what we need, but stay firm: witch hearts want what they want. Being upfront with yourself about how you express and experience love will help you recognize people who operate the same way as you—and help you stay compassionate and communicative if you fall for someone who operates differently.

▶ ▶ ▶ Don't get *too* dreamy.

Like many powerful forms of magic, there's a flip side to this conjuring practice. Resist the urge to become so absurdly devoted to this imaginary person that real people have no hope of measuring up. Instead, let the ideal partner act as a beacon, a reminder that "good enough" isn't good enough—that you can move toward something you truly want instead of merely dodging the worst.

Focus on What You Want

If you're having a hard time figuring out what matters to you in a romantic relationship, this spell will help you focus on the positive feelings you hope to get from a potential partner.

WHAT YOU'LL NEED:

A bathtub or your bed

4 small pieces of paper

A comfortable glove or shoe

A piece of food you find delicious

You can do this ritual anytime, but it works especially well if you have a date coming up. Fill the bathtub and immerse yourself, or lie in the bed. Focus on the sensation of being cradled and supported. Get out of the bath (and dry off) or get up from the bed, and repeat the following incantation:

As now, so forever. As alone, so with others.

After you've said the incantation, fold one piece of paper three times to seal that feeling.

Put on the glove or shoe. Focus on how it fits comfortably without constricting, chafing, or binding. Repeat the incantation, and then fold the second piece of paper to seal the feeling.

Do seven jumping jacks (or seven sit-ups, or seven cartwheels, or seven reps of whatever physical activity is comfortable for you). Focus on the sense of being energized and excited. Repeat the incantation a third time, and fold the third piece of paper.

Slowly eat the food. Focus on the feeling of being pleased and nourished. Repeat the incantation once last time, and fold the final piece of paper.

After the date (or the next day, if you don't have a date planned), hold the folded pieces of paper between your hands close to your heart. Contemplate the feelings of support, comfort, energy, and pleasure that you are able to access on your own. Consider whether you experience these same feelings when in the presence of the other person, or whether any conflicts prevent you from being supported, comfortable, energized, or happy in the ways you are by yourself. Keep the papers inside a diary or favorite book so you can check in with these feelings in the future.

The Waxing and Waning of Desire

WHAT TO DO WHEN YOU DON'T WANT TO HAVE SEX

~~~

Some witches believe in white and black magic not as performances of good and evil but as representations of magical energy. White magic is done when your energy is high, when you feel loved and happy and fulfilled, and it creates more of those feelings in the world. Black magic is performed out of fear and anger, a final thrashing of panic in order to survive, and it creates more fear and uncertainty.

This has to do with sex, we promise.

When Jaya was 12, she felt like the last person in the world who hadn't kissed anyone. Her friends had started going on dates and were making out in movie theaters, and, once they realized she was being left out, they huddled together and schemed over which boy they could convince to initiate her. Which basically made her want to die.

Jaya would eventually get her first kiss, and many more, but what plagued her then wasn't just that nobody seemed to want to kiss her. It was that, if she really thought about it, she didn't feel like kissing, either. There was a bud of sexuality inside her and she knew that, someday, it would bloom. But she wasn't ready for sex. Not yet. And she found it annoying as hell that her friends thought that was weird.

Growing up, most of us are bombarded with conflicting messages about sexual behavior. On one hand, it's what our species is designed to do, and we're treated as if there's something wrong with us if we don't want it. But on the other, we're not supposed to want it too much, or want it at the wrong times, or consider it supremely important. Many people get angry at these mixed messages and let that anger provoke a reaction.

But by reacting with energizing white magic instead of damaging black magic, we can neutralize both kinds of pressure and relieve our anger at the source. Here are some places the black magic can get you, and the white magic you can do to get it off your back.

▶ ▶ ▶ When you're single and happy

Black Magic: Caving to pressure to couple up by going on unfulfilling, unwanted dates. Assuming that being romantic is the only way to be social and becoming a hermit in response.

White Magic: Finding romance-free ways of being social, like seeing friends and family or joining clubs. Deflecting about your dating life by talking up all your activities and interests. Showing the people around you how fulfilling single life can be.

▶ ▶ ▶ When you crave physicality but don't want a partner

Black Magic: Dating someone you don't like just for the cuddles and orgasms.

White Magic: Seeking friends who appreciate a little physical affection, like hugs or couch snuggles. Getting a massage. Spending all the money you're saving on dates on sex toys.

▶ ▶ ▶ When you're in a romantic relationship but aren't feeling a spark

Black Magic: Staying silent out of fear that your partner will be mad at you.

White Magic: Being open about your feelings and working together to find a solution. Are there things you and your partner can do to remain physical that you still feel comfortable with? Is this a sign of deeper issues within the relationship? Whatever the answer, addressing the situation will be much more nourishing than pretending it's not happening.

▶ ▶ ▶ When you want a romantic relationship but don't want sex

Black Magic: Pretending you want sex to attract someone, who will inevitably feel disappointed when they learn the truth.

White Magic: Being upfront about your wants, and knowing that whoever comes into your life will be there because they know and accept you.

One final note: Given that many a witch and woman has been punished for thinking, talking about, or (gasp) having sex at the wrong times, or for enjoying it too much, it's easy to conflate an embrace of your inner witch with an embrace of sexual promiscuity. Throwing away the shackles of sexual oppression is not the same as performing aggressive sexuality. Rejecting those expectations assumes you have sexual desires that need releasing in the first place, and maybe you don't—and rejecting for rejection's sake can quickly become a draining form of black magic. Making sexual choices for yourself, not to conform to or rebel against anyone else's ideas, is what creates power. In turn, the beneficial white magic comes from acting on what you want, whether that's freely accepting who you're attracted to or finally admitting that you're not at all interested in sex. Whatever the answer, you're no less magic.

FLIRTING WITH RUNES

Runes are letters from ancient Germanic alphabets that are thought by many to possess magical charms. Casting runes can supposedly tell you about your future, or at least symbolize deep truths that mere words cannot reveal.

You know what else are cool-looking symbols that can say more than words? Emoji.

Witches are skilled at utilizing the deeper powers of glyphs and marks, whether by recognizing multiple meanings in a single symbol (for instance, if you text your crush an eggplant emoji, you're probably not trying to suggest stir-fry for dinner) or simply by getting the person on the other end to pick up on the vibes.

Here's how to use these modern-day runes to reveal deep truths while texting your crush.

▸ ▸ ▸ Food

The food emoji are some of the most sensual: eating involves our mouths and our hands, and some food emoji look suspiciously like certain body parts. But if you don't want to get as "explicit" as texting a banana or a peach, you have lots of other options. An ice cream swirl or lollipop are cute and sweet, and nothing says "I want to devour you" like a fork and a knife. Followed by a playful wink, of course.

▸ ▸ ▸ Animals

Animal familiars are often used by witches for spying. Their familiar can hide in plain sight, gathering information about enemies, and relay it to their witch without anyone being the wiser. If an emoji exists of your animal familiar, text it to your crush and see if it elicits any new information about their deeper feelings. Or if it sparks a conversation about why on earth you just texted them a snake.

▸ ▸ ▸ People

The dancing woman may be the flirtiest emoji out there, and depending on how you use her, she can mean either "I'm here to have fun!" or "BOY, BYE." Images of people kissing can reveal your inner intentions, once you're on that level, and lips or a tongue can reveal even more.

▸ ▸ ▸ Spooky Things

The skull, candle, or crystal ball emoji can help you slowly reveal your darker side and also determine who spooks too easily to be worth your time. If you want to imply that you laughed yourself to death at a joke, text your crush a laughing face next to a coffin. If you're exhausted from studying, send a book and a skull.

▸ ▸ ▸ Hearts

Use the hearts to cast spells corresponding to their colors: for instance, red to inspire passion and sex, or pink for friendship. Yellow can inspire a deeper mental connection, while green gives vibes of good luck and harmony. It's up to you which of those emotions you want to be the catalyst of your connection—just don't use the broken heart unless you mean it.

▸ ▸ ▸ Random Symbols

The lesser-used characters of the emoji alphabet offer lots of creative possibilities. A gift box might symbolize that you've got a surprise waiting. The thought bubble can mean that you're thinking of your intended. And the "no one under 18" symbol could be a heads-up that you're about to say some very grown-up things.

The Magic Circle of Consent

〰️

Witch spells can't universally protect you against people who don't respect your desires, but your personal relationship with witchery can help remind you that, at every moment in every encounter, your consent matters.

We often talk about consent as if it's something handed over at a particular moment, when in fact it's something two (or more) people build together over the course of a relationship, however brief or lengthy that relationship might be. Consent isn't just something you grant or deny, it's also something you manifest, in the way that you manifest your will when performing a magical ritual. We think *will* is probably a better word than *consent*—consent implies giving in to something or someone, whereas will is more about actively wanting something and making it happen. Sex shouldn't be something you merely agree to; it should be something you will into being with your partner(s). (As the Wiccans say, "if it harm none, do what thou wilt." Do what you *will*, not just what you agree to!)

Many rituals begin with a kind of traditional magic circle, the symbolic space created (often with salt or chalk, as on page 101). Standing inside the circle may offer protection or allow a witch to tap into and contain magical energy. But magic circles are fragile and should be exited carefully; breaking the circle disrupts the spell. Sexual consent—or sexual will—operates much the same way. Working with your partner, you can inscribe a metaphorical circle of safety and energy around your encounter, which collapses if it's not maintained.

▶ ▶ ▶ Drawing the circle

You may want to draw the circle verbally, by asking your partner what they want to do or requesting permission, but of course manifesting consent doesn't have to be a formal exchange. Listen carefully, tune in to signals of enjoyment and enthusiasm, and signal your own desires clearly. But make things explicit if necessary—if you're not sure they're having fun, ask! If you're uncomfortable or you want something to change, say so! Talking will only strengthen the circle, not break it.

▶ ▶ ▶ Working the magic

A strong circle of consent, once drawn, can be self-sustaining. Instead of keeping your wits about you, constantly checking in to make sure that everyone is having fun, a firm circle lets you get a little more heedless. In fact, sex is used in a lot of magical practice specifically precisely because it has this power to remove your self-consciousness and ego—you *should* feel like you're able to let go. Nevertheless, it's important not to let the circle become an impermeable barrier: when you move on to a new activity, check back in momentarily with yourself and your partner. Everything still good? Then feel free to get lost again.

▶ ▶ ▶ Breaking the circle

As with any cooperative magic, the moment one of you taps out, the spell of consent—of will—is broken. One person alone cannot create this circle, but one person can—and should be able to, if they choose—destroy it; it exists only as long as you're both willing it into existence. With any luck, the circle will disappear naturally after everyone's satisfied with the encounter, but sometimes the spell is broken before you (or your partner) anticipates. The key is to notice this crucial moment and not to ignore it—persisting despite a collapsed magic circle is a recipe for negative energy at best or emotional and physical damage at worst.

If the circle and your connection with your partner are strong, you may feel able to speak up in no uncertain terms when one of you wants to break the spell. But unlike many spells, this magic circle can dissolve without an explicit command. To use this magic responsibly, both you and your partner should also be attuned to nonverbal and physical signals—if the other person feels tense or resistant, that's a good sign that the circle has disappeared. You may want to talk about it afterward, or you may prefer to conclude and part ways without obligation.

Yes and No

WHAT YOU'LL NEED:

This visualization focuses your mind on the innate, elemental power we all exercise when saying "yes" and saying "no."

A quiet room or outdoor space

A full bathtub, sink, glass, or natural body of water

A candle

Your "yes" and "no" are already powerful. Even leaving aside everything they can do for you outside the bedroom, they're the only thing—not someone else's feelings, not what you "should" do, not what everyone else is doing—that should determine what kind of sex you have, and when, and with whom.

Sit or lie in a comfortable position, close your eyes, and concentrate on your heartbeat. Picture yourself as an immovable wall with a door set in it that only you can open and close. When you're ready, say these words:

In earth, in water, in air, in fire
I am the master of my desire

As you say the incantation, picture a ball of green light and energy collecting around your right hand and a ball of red light and energy around your left.

Raise your right hand, and say aloud, "Yes." Picture the green light shooting forth and emitting waves of pressure in the air. Raise your left hand, and say aloud, "No." Picture the red light doing the same.

Touch your right hand to the floor or ground, and say aloud, "Yes." Picture the green light shaking the earth like a tiny quake. Touch your left hand to the floor or ground, and say aloud, "No." Picture the red light doing the same.

Repeat the incantation, focusing on the water; as you say "yes" and "no," imagine the surface rippling like the glass of water in *Jurassic Park*.

Repeat the incantation again, focusing on the candle, and imagine it guttering and flickering in response to the power of your "yes" and "no."

Say the incantation once again, and picture the red and green lights receding from your hands into your body, where it will stay until you need to use it.

Choosing the "Broomstick" for You

~~~

The image of a witch riding a broomstick has a secret meaning . . . which is pretty obvious when you think about it. A woman straddling a long, hard object is a threat not just because she can spit on you from the sky. She's a threat because she's straddling a long, hard object.

Modern Western society is still generally uncomfortable with masturbation, so imagine how uncomfortable we were in the days when the dominant culture was so strongly religious that witch hunts were considered a social good. For many, the idea that a woman could feel complete by herself, without a man, was shocking and shameful. (Honestly, for many, it still is.) The broomstick symbolized the heretical act of a woman taking physical pleasure into—literally—her own hands.

The witch on her broomstick is proud, not ashamed, of her body, and she doesn't need to ask permission to tap into her sexuality. Orgasms are serious big-time magic—it's no coincidence that many occult traditions incorporate sex rituals, and some occult scholars even believe you can harness orgasmic energy and use it like a battery—and the witch wields that power all on her own. (Of course, toys—a broomstick or an easily cleaned silicone equivalent—can be used with a partner. But you can use them alone if you don't have a partner, if your partner isn't around, if you're tapping into the power of orgasm for a practical spell, if you really want to freak out a Puritan, or for whatever reason you like.)

You don't know for sure which sex toys will work for you until you try them out, and many are too expensive for much comparison shopping. Figuring out what sensations you like can help you narrow down your options. (All of these can be used regardless of your anatomy, though some may be better suited to people with a vagina. We're omitting toys that are designed to be penetrated, both because those aren't as universally useful and because the broomstick metaphor has to be good for *something*.)

▸ ▸ ▸ The Elfin Wand

Some people want a lot of control over where they direct sensations. A small vibrator is perfect for this, and some can be strapped onto your finger, so you don't have to worry about hanging on to something small and fiddly. If you have a vagina and also enjoy penetration, many penetrative vibrators have a little external prong that delivers focused vibration, though it's harder to direct than smaller nonpenetrative options. For extra control, choose a vibe with multiple speed settings.

▸ ▸ ▸ The Thunder Goddess

If you prefer a more distributed, strong vibration, which covers more ground but is less easily directed, you may want a vibrating wand with a large head. These aren't designed for penetration but can be used in combination with a G-spot or prostate toy. They're great for people who find very focused sensations distracting or even painful. Try to find one with multiple speeds, because the really powerful wands are . . . well, really powerful. Vulva-havers who have a hard time reaching orgasm report that the classic Hitachi magic wand can work wonders, but some feel that Hitachi vibrations are too strong to be sexy.

▸ ▸ ▸ The Devil's Finger

Though G-spot (for vagina-havers) or prostate (for prostate-havers) stimulation doesn't always lead directly to orgasm, it can significantly enhance your experience. Every body is different, so figure out where your spot is manually before you go shopping, so you can get a toy with the right proportions. Pay attention to what kind of stimulation does the trick for you; some toys with targeted penetration also vibrate, and others don't. You may find that vibration is key, or that it's too weak and you prefer a toy that is rubbed or rocked against the target spot.

Or, if nothing but an actual literal enchanted flying machine will suit your needs, you can do what historical witches reportedly did: ask for help from demons.

WITCH HISTORY

THE ORIGINS OF THE MAGIC BROOMSTICK

POPULAR IMAGES OF WITCHES depict them soaring through the sky on broomsticks to terrorize innocent townspeople (or play quidditch). But if a witch is powerful enough to fly on her own, why the arbitrary accessory? Just where did the broomstick come from?

The answer boils down to the two major themes of witch paranoia—drugs and sex. Humans have long experimented with hallucinogenic plants. As John Mann writes in *Murder, Magic, and Medicine,* humans discovered in medieval times not only that eating things like deadly nightshade and mandrake may make you intensely nauseated, but also that absorbing them through the skin, especially the thinner mucus membranes, produced effects that are significantly . . . trippier. Psychedelic self-medication figured in some of the earliest accounts of witches with brooms: in 1324, an investigation of Lady Alice Kyteler for witchcraft produced a "Pipe of oyntment, wherewith she greased a staffe, upon which she ambled and galloped through thick and thin," according to Robert C. Fuller in *Stairways to Heaven: Drugs in American Religious History.* Brooms were a handy way to get that "oyntment" flowing through your body.

However, the notion of witches flying on broomsticks didn't come for another three hundred years or so. Between 1668 and 1675, hundreds of women in Sweden were accused of stealing children on the Sabbath to worship the Devil. According to child witnesses, the women would make their escape by flying on poles. Reports of these Swedish trials went the seventeenth-century equivalent of viral. Soon thereafter, the Puritan townspeople of Salem, Massachusetts, began to accuse witches of flying, which the witches themselves corroborated. In *Farther Account of the Tryals of the New-England Witches*, minister and witch-hunter Cotton Mather wrote that one Martha Carrier "confessed that the Devil carried them on a pole." Other members of Carrier's family were charged with flying, and according to another account, cited in Stacy Schiff's *The Witches*, nearly seventy witches descended on a meadow flying on various poles.

By 1711, poles had given way to classic witchy brooms. In his *History of the Ridiculous Extravagancies of Monsieur Oufle*, published that year, the French abbot and philosopher Laurent Bordelon balks at the supposed power of witches: "What probability is there, that as often as a silly old Woman is pleased to mutter two or three Words out of the Grimoire, or Black-Book, and clap a Broom betwixt her Legs, that Satan should be oblig'd to transport her thro' the Chirney whither she pleases?" (Good question.)

Although we can't be sure what prompted the switch from pole to broom in the popular imagination of the witch-fearing public, there are a few theories about the connection between unruly women and sweeping implements. Jumping on brooms was part of some Pagan planting rituals, and a broom may have seemed like a suspiciously convenient place for a witch to conceal a wand (pretty much every preindustrial woman had a broom, after all—it'd be a great hiding spot). Regardless of the origins of the association, some modern-day Wiccans have chosen to incorporate brooms into their (non-transport-related) magical work, especially (fittingly!) for spells of cleansing and purification—because nothing is more magical than chores.

Saying the Magic Words in Bed

~~~

We talk a lot in this book about the power of speaking your goals and desires out loud, and nowhere is this power more important than in the bedroom. But that doesn't make verbalizing during intimacy easy: we may absorb the idea that good girls don't talk about naughty things, or that only pushy women ask for what they want. Such fast-acting incantations may take a little practice.

Here are a few topics of bedroom communication and some magic words you can practice saying to get the conversation going.

▶ ▶ ▶ Pleasure

"What feels good" is the most obvious topic to talk about when you're engaged in an activity that's supposed to make both of you feel good. Because bodies are so varied, and what feels pleasurable to someone else might not suit you, communication is the *only* way to have truly satisfying sex. You don't have to jump right to graduate-level dirty talk, but practicing a few key phrases will help you feel more confident directing the action.

Magic words: "I want you." "That feels good." "Faster." "Slower."

▶ ▶ ▶ Pain

Women are often taught to be "polite" about sex, and sometimes in intimate situations we avoid speaking up about discomfort that keeps us from fully enjoying ourselves. Maybe your partner is leaning on you painfully, or you're falling off the bed, or you don't think having your boob honked is sexy—but you think mentioning it would ruin the moment. We promise: it won't. You never have to put up with unpleasantness, pain, or even minor discomfort just to avoid awkwardness.

Magic words: "Can you move a little?" "That hurts." "Don't do that." "Gentler, please."

▸ ▸ ▸ Contraception and STI prevention

We don't have to tell you how important it is to use protection during sex. But we can give you permission to be *really annoying* about it, if you want to be—even if doing so is awkward, even if it ruins the moment, even if it gets on people's nerves. Insist on a condom if you want to, even if you're already on the Pill or have an IUD. If you can get pregnant, don't hesitate to tell a partner who can get people pregnant your views on abortion before anything goes down. And if your method of protection isn't working for you, you can—and should—stick up for yourself, both with partners and with medical professionals. Recent research has shown that hormonal birth control is linked with depression in a way doctors have long ignored, and there are other side effects that doctors may not take seriously. Put your foot down if you need to.

Magic words: "When were you last tested?" "You'll need a condom." "These side effects are not okay with me and I need an alternative."

A SPELL FOR

Talking about Sex

This spell will help you admit your wants and needs to yourself and verbalize any dormant feeling you may have.

WHAT YOU'LL NEED:

A white candle

Matches

Thyme, fresh or dried

A small red envelope

Once, Jaya hired a witch to cast a spell on her marriage. On Etsy, you can find no shortage of self-described witches promising to make someone love you or offering to hex your ex. So, after blithely sending her full name and birthday to a stranger on the internet (don't do this, folks!) Jaya received confirmation of the spell a week later: photos of her and her husband's names written on a red envelope full of herbs as it was burned over a candle, presumably with a witch behind the camera chanting for the magical sex they would soon be having.

So, did it work? Sort of. After the spell was cast, Jaya felt a palpable sexual energy (she didn't tell her husband what she had done), and their interactions were great. But around the same time they both caught a horrible stomach virus.

To avoid any adverse results, we recommend this at-home version of the spell. Try doing it on a Tuesday or a Friday. Tuesday is ruled by Mars, who rules over sex and lust, and Friday by Venus, who rules over love and passion.

Light the candle and sit in front of it, and take a moment to focus on the flame. Then hold the thyme between your fingers and in front of your face. Start rubbing the thyme in your fingers, enough so that you begin to smell it strongly.

Once the herb releases its scent, rub it on the center of your forehead, your lips, and your chest. Breathe deeply, and picture twin paths of light traveling from your head and your heart to your lips. With every breath, imagine those paths growing brighter and stronger, drawing your thoughts and feelings out of your brain and heart (respectively) and toward your mouth.

Breathe this way until you feel the connections getting stronger. Then place the remaining thyme in the envelope and carry it with you for at least a week. Whenever you find yourself thinking of sex, hold the envelope in your hands, remembering those paths to your mouth to encourage your thoughts and feelings to flow smoothly.

WITCH HISTORY

WITCHES AND
REPRODUCTIVE
FREEDOM

IN 1484, INNOCENT VIII issued a papal bull authorizing church inquisitors to investigate claims of witchcraft. The bull was written at the request of Inquisitor Heinrich Kramer, who would go on to cowrite the *Malleus Maleficarum*—the explicitly misogynistic witch-hunting guide. Kramer believed there had been an outbreak of witchcraft in Germany and wanted permission to prosecute it to the fullest extent of his power.

The papal bull granted that permission. It officially recognized the existence of witches and described their crimes, some of which it explicitly related to sex, abortion, and contraception: witches "have slain infants yet in the mother's womb," and they "hinder men from performing the sexual act and women from conceiving."

The *Malleus Maleficarum* talks about witches preventing conception and causing abortions—or, when those failed, eating babies or offering them to the devil. The authors recognize that not all contraception is witch-induced: "a man can by natural means, such as herbs ... procure that a woman cannot generate or conceive." When a woman does it, though? There's something real suspicious about that.

As John M. Riddle writes in *Eve's Herbs: A History of Contraception and Abortion in the West*, women have been finding ways to limit childbearing since basically the dawn of civilization. Often they used brute force, either by blocking the cervix to prevent impregnation with a device similar to a modern diaphragm made of wool or bamboo (or another material available in a pre-industrial society), or by inducing miscarriage through physical exertion or applying pressure to the abdomen. Ancient Egyptians made a kind of contraceptive sponge out of honey, dates, plant matter, and acacia gum (which breaks down into lactic acid, an ingredient used in modern spermicides). In ancient Greece, a midwife might have administered silphium, a fennel-like herb that was so effective an abortifacient that demand for its use may have led to its extinction. Herbs like pennyroyal and Queen Anne's lace are still occasionally used to induce abortion today, though they are neither safe nor reliable.

None of these contraceptive methods require actual magical power, of course; they're just science, folklore, or often a little of both. But for the Catholic Church and its agents, women controlling their reproduction was inherently devilish. By assigning malign motives to contraception and abortion, they condemned women's bodily autonomy.

Well, fine. If birth control and abortion are witchcraft, then all women (and all people with uteruses) should get to be witches. Eating babies is a problem, but otherwise, we get complete control over what we do with our wombs—and no inquisitor can tell us otherwise.

Feel Sexually Powerful

WHAT YOU'LL NEED:

An outfit that makes you feel powerful (optional)

A bathroom or wall mirror

A plush blanket

A red candle

Matches

This is not a spell to create sexual attraction, but rather one to make you feel more in touch with your sexuality. If others pick up on that, well, that's just a great bonus.

First, put on your outfit. (Alternatively, be naked. This and most spells work great when performed unclothed.) Next, look at yourself in the mirror. Pose, move, maybe take a selfie or two, whatever it takes for you to recognize your body and start enjoying what you see. Then lay the blanket on the floor and light the candle. Lie down on the blanket and place the candle on the floor just above your head. (Make sure it's in a candleholder or other sturdy base to keep it from falling over.)

Close your eyes, keeping the image of yourself in the mirror in your mind's eye. Start moving your hands up and down your body, being aware of every inch of your skin and how it feels against the fabric and the blanket. Then let your mind drift to your sexual desires. If you don't know what you desire, use your imagination to put yourself in different sexual situations. How does it feel? What do you find that interests you?

Breathe deeply as your body starts to feel warmer. When you're ready, recite the following three times:

My body is fire
And I am deserving
Of all my desires

Slowly get up and blow out the candle. Sleep under that blanket that night.

Accepting Singleness

When you're single, even if you're lonely, you are whole and you're not alone. This ritual will help you be patient with others and kind to yourself if you're seeking love and not finding it.

WHAT YOU'LL NEED:

A tarot deck

The idea of the balanced pair is important to a lot of spiritual and magical systems: the dark and light, the yin and yang. But singularity also has magical significance. We greatly value things we have only one of, things that are indivisible and irreplaceable: the sun, the earth, our bodies.

Remove the following cards from the deck and stack them in this order: the Lovers, the Hermit, the Fool, the Magician, either the High Priestess or the Hierophant (choose based on preference, gender identity, or coin toss), either the Empress or the Emperor (ditto), the Chariot, the Star, the Moon, the Sun, the World, Strength, Justice, Temperance, Judgment, the Wheel of Fortune.

Lay the Lovers and the Hermit in front of you. The Lovers will represent partnership and couplehood. The Hermit will represent who you are when you're solitary.

Then contemplate each of the cards in turn before placing it on the Hermit. For the Fool, think about your sense of humor and wonder. For the Magician, think about your knowledge and intelligence. For the High Priestess or the Hierophant, think about your wisdom and morality. For the Empress or the Emperor, think about your leadership qualities. For the Chariot, think about travel and adventures you've had or are planning. For the Star, think about your connection with the spiritual or the scientific. For the Moon, think about personal sensitivity and connection to your body. For the Sun, think about the radiance of your personality. For the World, think about your goals. For Strength, Justice, Temperance, and Judgment, think about each of those qualities. These represent the qualities you possess whether you're single or coupled, the qualities that make you whole.

When you reach the Wheel of Fortune, place it on top of the Lovers. This represents the only thing you have while in a couple that you don't have on your own: the luck to have encountered someone compatible.

The ritual is complete. You may reshuffle the tarot deck to use again. If you don't plan to use it for a while, though, you may want to keep the cards you assigned to the Hermit in an accessible place like a bedside table, to look through if you feel down.

Healing a Broken Heart

WHAT YOU'LL NEED:

This spell reenacts the experience of letting someone deeper and deeper into your heart and then helps you close the exit wound gently, bit by bit.

A picture or drawing of your former beloved

A jar

A rose

Scissors

Heartbreak is so agonizing because it infiltrates every part of your life. You reevaluate your opinion of yourself—are you less worthy and lovable than you'd thought? You are forced to reimagine your days—all the time you used to spend with someone else feels empty and meaningless. You let go of all your visions of what your future would be like and face the void of a life without the other person. It destabilizes your daily life, your confidence, your plans, and your sense of identity. A centering ritual can be the first step to reclaiming stability.

Sit on the floor or ground in a quiet, secluded space with little or no breeze. Lean forward and place the picture on the ground as far away from you as you can reach. Place the jar at your side.

Pluck the outer petals off the rose and lay them around you in a semicircle, with at least a foot of space between the petals and your body. Move the picture just inside the semicircle.

Pluck the next layer of petals off the rose and lay them around you in a semicircle closer to you than the previous semicircle. Move the picture just inside this new semicircle. Repeat once more, making a third semi-circle and placing the picture right in front of you.

Hold the heart of the rose between your hands, close to your heart, and concentrate on all the qualities you possess that have nothing to do with the person you lost. What do you love doing by yourself? What are you like when they're not around? What essential qualities are inherent to you and unchanged by your heartbreak? Place the heart of the rose in the jar.

Collect the petals from the innermost semicircle, and move the picture to just inside the second semicircle. As you pick up the petals, think about the positive aspects of having your living space to yourself, exactly the way you want it. Put the petals in the jar.

Collect the petals from the next semicircle, and move the picture to just inside the final semicircle. As you pick up the petals, think about the strongest parts of your social life without your former flame—spending time with friends, clubs you belong to, and activities you like doing on your own. Put the petals in the jar.

Collect the petals from the outermost semicircle, and again place the picture as far away as you can reach. As you pick up the petals, think about positive plans for your future that do not involve the person you've lost. Do you have a trip coming up, or can you plan a solo journey in the near future? Are you poised for a success in work or school? Put the petals in the jar.

With the scissors, cut the picture into three parts and bury it in the ground, in a flowerpot, or in a trash can. Keep the jar of petals until you feel stronger, and then scatter the dried petals in a place that is meaningful to you but where your former beloved has never set foot.

BANISHMENT

THE POWER TO AVOID WHAT BRINGS YOU DOWN

Fairy tales paint witches as consorts of the devil, vengeful agents of chaos intent on ruining the lives of those who cross them (or those who don't, if the mood strikes) with devilish magic. But in these stories the witch is hardly a hero; her adversaries always win. From Medusa to the Wicked Witch of the West, many a fictional witch has met her end thanks to a mob of townspeople, a heroic prince, an innocent princess, or even her own demonic sidekick.

These days, we're more likely to face down a metaphorical adversary than a literal one. Demons wielding pointy emotional pitchforks arrive at our doors every day: friends or lovers whose demands for love and loyalty conceal toxic motives, or a family member whose affection is conditional on our silence about our experiences, our opinions, or our true selves. Sometimes the demons scuttle into our brains even though we try to block them out. Sometimes they arrive in disguise, and we welcome them into our lives again and again without realizing. And sometimes we recognize them, but we welcome them in just the same.

Though we might think of magic powers as a way to transform external circumstances, they can be even stronger when used for protection against the negative internal demons caused by the world around us (and the people in it). Recognizing—and then eliminating—these damaging inner forces is classic magic: banishment. Banishment is also about empowering yourself so that you can stop those demons from plaguing you. More than just learning to say "no" (although that's an important skill we'll be talking about), this type of banishment is a holistic form of self-care.

The trick, as with many forms of magic, is to find a balance. Self-care can easily turn into self-indulgence, which can become a wellspring of negative energy, and recognizing the difference between the two is the heavy lifting of the banishment practice. For example, sitting on the couch eating ice cream every day may feel good because your life is stressful and ice cream is delicious, but it's not a good long-term solution. No matter how blissed out you are on sugar, a voice in your head is telling you to take a walk, read a book, or at least invite a friend over to share the ice cream with you. But that voice gets quieter in more difficult situations, especially when your toxic feelings of self-defeat and worthlessness come swirling up.

Your adversaries and inner demons will come for you. There's little magic that will change that. This chapter will help you confront them, protect yourself against their powers, be strong enough to fight back, and learn to grieve. You can teach yourself to rise above the mob when the pitchforks knock at your door, and you can learn to calm the demons when they rise inside you. The witches of fairy tales may have been tricked by those who hated them, but real witches get to defeat their own demons.

Expelling Social Toxicity

HOW TO CURE YOUR ALLERGY
TO PEOPLE WHO SUCK

━━∿∿━━

Witches were the original healers—"the unlicensed doctors and anatomists of western history," as Barbara Ehrenreich and Deirdre English put it in *Witches, Midwives, and Nurses: A History of Women Healers.* The witch had to be a bit of a scientist, keenly observing which remedies helped, which ones harmed, and which ones didn't do anything much. And when it comes to self-care like food, sleep, and beauty treatments, a lot of us keep up that empirical tradition. Think of all the times you or your friends have said things like "I get so hungry by noon if I have anything sugary in the morning," "Oil cleansing makes my skin go crazy," or "If I nap for longer than 20 minutes, I'll be a zombie."

Rarely, though, do we apply that same scrutiny to the way we feel around other people. If a food reliably makes us sick or tired, we quit eating it. But if a particular person makes us feel crummy every time we interact with them, we often think, "Maybe I'm just not trying hard enough."

Nobody wants to hurt someone else's feelings, and women in particular are socialized to be obliging. But you also have a limited amount of mental and social energy—wasting it on people who bring you down is like being lactose intolerant but eating so much cheese every day that you're too full for anything else. (Okay, that sounds wonderful, but you can see how it wouldn't be the greatest idea.) It'll only leave you feeling worse—and leave less room for something nutritive.

So how do you figure out which people bring you down and then limit the effect they have on you? Doctor Witch might prescribe the same thing that healers recommend for diagnosing sensitivities: an elimination diet, followed by gradual reintroduction. And, if necessary, careful avoidance, plus soothing remedies to help you when avoidance is impossible.

▸ ▸ ▸ Elimination

How long can you reasonably go without seeing this person? The answer depends on your situation; you can't avoid your boss for as long as you can a casual acquaintance or a parent who lives out of state. Pick a plausible time period, and avoid that person consciously and deliberately throughout. Notice your reactions during this "detox." How do you feel when they're not around? Did you relax as soon as you gave yourself permission not to talk to them for a while? Conversely, do you miss them or regret their absence?

▸ ▸ ▸ Reintroduction

After your elimination period, plan a controlled, finite exposure to the person—something where you have an excuse to leave after a set span of time. Notice how you feel after interacting with them, compared to how you felt during the elimination period. If you immediately feel tired, bummed out, annoyed, angry, self-critical, or some other negative emotion—and you weren't feeling that way previously—you may have isolated this person as the source of your mental funk. So what to do now? There are two options: avoidance and fortification.

▸ ▸ ▸ Avoidance

Unless you truly think that this person is unwittingly doing a specific hurtful thing—and that calling them on it will make them stop—there's no reason to tell the person explicitly what they're doing wrong. You are under no obligation to explain that you don't want to hang out because their attitude makes you feel bad. Sometimes people just don't mesh, and gently drifting apart is an adequate (and less aggressive) solution. Give yourself permission to decline invitations or requests, firmly but nonspecifically: "Sorry, I won't be able to!" No further explanation needed.

▸ ▸ ▸ Fortification

If there are aspects of the acquaintance that you still value—for instance, if you're happy spending time with the person in a group, but not one on one—perform the boundaries spell on page 101 to insulate yourself against their negative effects. If this is a person you can't avoid, don't despair—you just need the mental magic equivalent of Lactaid to tolerate their toxic crap. Designate a preventative "treatment" for when you can't avoid them. For instance, if it's a coworker or a boss, keep a bowl of M&Ms on your desk and take one when you're forced to encounter the person. As you chew, tell yourself, "I am fortified and strong." Give yourself permission to end the encounter as swiftly as you can, before the remedy wears off.

Move through Loss

WHAT YOU'LL NEED:

Remember, the opposite of loss is creation. Use this act of creativity to acknowledge all your feelings, and start the process of moving through them.

A photo or memento of the person or thing you're mourning

Tape

Black, white, and red string

Sometimes, there is no such thing as a quick fix. When you're experiencing loss and grief (and not just following a death; this could be the toll of someone leaving your life), only time and, well, feeling your feelings will make you feel better. Still, the stages of grief—denial, anger, bargaining, depression, and acceptance—do not happen linearly. You may feel them all at once, or you may think you've hit acceptance only to find yourself angry moments later. This ritual will help you calm and center yourself in the storm of grief.

Place the photo or memento on the table in front of you. Tape the ends of the three pieces of string to the table's edge, and begin braiding them.

As you braid, contemplate what each of the three colors represents: black for death, white for life, and red for rebirth. Voice every feeling that comes to you, no matter how simple. If none come to mind, ask yourself these questions to get your thoughts flowing: Do you miss this person or thing? Do you feel guilty that you don't miss them? Are you angry that they're gone or that they weren't kinder to you? Are you scared of what will happen next?

When you've finished braiding, knot each end of the braid while speaking the name of the person, animal, or concept you're mourning. Tie your new bracelet around your wrist and wear it for a week. Then cut it off, wrap it around the photo or memento you used while making it, and store in an envelope or box wherever you keep things safe.

The Dark Magic of Emotional Abuse

HOW TO REDISCOVER YOUR STRENGTH

~~~

Being in an emotionally abusive relationship can feel like living under a curse. An abusive partner has the power to rewrite your sense of reality—to convince you that they're the only one who could love you, that you're helpless without them, that you're crazy for objecting to how they treat you, that they'll change.

Even the most powerful witches are susceptible to the dark wizardry of abuse. There's no shame in being enchanted or imprisoned, but you must—and can—escape. Truly overthrowing this evil magic, not to mention recognizing the full scope of its effect, can take all your powers and the powers of your coven. If you're in immediate danger, don't try to tough it out with magic. Call on family, friends, or therapists to help, or call the National Domestic Violence Hotline at 1-800-799-SAFE.

After you end such a relationship, the curse tends to linger. You may hear your abuser's voice in your head long after they're gone, or find yourself seeking out similarly destructive situations because you've been enchanted to believe you don't deserve better. A ritual can help you solidify a clearer state of mind and banish the aftereffects of your past relationship so that you can make room in your life for positive friends and partners. Here are some abusive spells that can have long-lasting effects and quick, silent counterspells that can help clear away those toxic feelings for good.

▶ ▶ ▶ Illusion

Abusers conjure phantoms—and can even convince you that you can see them, too. They may be jealous of imaginary rivals ("Why were you talking to your coworker for so long last night?") or blame imagined behavior for their emotions ("I wouldn't be so angry if you weren't being so irresponsible"). They may chastise you for things you haven't done, belittle you for decisions you didn't make, or overreact to "mistakes" that aren't serious.

Counterspell: Take a moment alone, if possible. Pass a hand over your face as if lifting a veil. (If you aren't alone, imagine yourself doing this action.) Find the most brightly colored or cleanest white object in your field of vision and fix your gaze on it. Then say in your head, "I see what I see, you cannot deceive me." If you wear glasses, contacts, or sunglasses, wear them while performing the ritual to charge them with this feeling of clarity. The next time you put them on, their stored power will enable you to fight back even harder against the abuser's fantasies that you've internalized.

▶ ▶ ▶ Binding

Abusers may try to make you financially or emotionally dependent upon them and may try to isolate you from your family and friends—so that you have no one else to lean on and no one to give you a reality check about your partner's behavior. Recovering relationships with loved ones and reestablishing a support network after the abuser is out of your life can be precarious and scary.

Counterspell: Envision an unbreakable cord of light extending from you to the people who love you. Anytime you recall your abuser convincing you to disconnect with those people, or saying that they don't love you, imagine tugging on the cord to send a signal: *Are you still with me?* Then imagine receiving a tug in reply: *Yes, I am.* To remind you of this unbreakable bond, keep a symbolic bit of string in your pocket or designate a necklace or bracelet for this purpose.

▶ ▶ ▶ Wall of Ice

Abusers may seek revenge for perceived slights or disobedience by freezing you out—pouting and sulking, giving you the silent treatment, withholding sex, or neglecting you emotionally. Even after you've chosen not to interact with them, the chill can remain for a long time afterward.

Counterspell: Turn the wall of ice into something you can control. Imagine the abuser's criticism and insults as a raging fire surrounding you. Breathe in for a count of five, and imagine the fire being blown away and extinguished by a freezing wind. Say in your head, "I thank you for the gift of your absence, and the space it has made for me."

▶ ▶ ▶ Mind Control

If you spend enough time being blamed, yelled at, mocked, insulted, criticized, or ignored, you may come to believe you deserve it—especially if you're socially isolated. Some abusers will even tell you outright that you're crazy or question your memory of events ("You never told me no") and it can feel impossible to put your perception to rights.

Counterspell: Hold your breath for a count of five, and imagine sinking down through shifting water and laying your hand on the solid ocean floor. Touch the nearest solid natural material (preferably stone or wood, although metal will do). If you can't do this without attracting attention, touch your own hand, elbow, or knee. Say in your head, "I am grounded and solid, I know what is true."

Abusers often cast self-perpetuating spells, enchanting you so that you'll keep casting the spell on yourself over and over, telling yourself that you're worthless and don't deserve better treatment even after you've escaped the relationship. These counterspells can help you fight that enchantment, but remember that you don't have to do it alone. If you ever need to draw on your coven (or outside help like a therapist or hotline), don't hesitate to do so.

The Joy of Hex

This symbolic hexing is for people in your life who've hurt you. It probably won't call down divine retribution for the wrong-doers, but it will provide emotional relief for you.

WHAT YOU'LL NEED:

A photo or drawing of the person you want to hex

A black candle

Matches

Hexing had a moment in the spotlight back in June 2016. When a judge sentenced Stanford University student Brock Turner to a mere six months in county jail for sexual assault—an appallingly light slap on the wrist that infuriated women everywhere, especially after the victim wrote a heart-rending letter about her experience—angry witches tried to even the scales the best way they knew how: with a mass hex.

A Facebook event titled "The Hexing of Brock Turner," created by a witch named Melanie Hexen, instructed would-be hexers to wrap a photo of Turner with a black string and then burn it in a black candle while reciting a spell that called for impotence, nightmares, and "constant pain of pine needles in your guts."

Did the hex cause Turner to suffer impotence and pine-needle gut pain in perpetuity? Probably not. But it gave the 600 or so women who RSVPed something active and symbolic to do about an outrageous miscarriage of justice that otherwise made them feel small and helpless. This symbolic hex, inspired by Hexen's ritual, can do the same for something in your personal life.

Hold or rest the picture in front of you, and say aloud the hurts and wrongs that the person has done. Address the picture directly, saying, "I accuse you," for each accusation.

Light the candle, saying, "What you have done to me, may it rebound on you tenfold. I curse you to suffer the consequences of your ugliness and cruelty." As the candle burns, picture the person getting smaller and smaller.

Carefully pick up the candle and drip black wax onto the picture. As you drip, say out loud, "I condemn you," one time for each of the accusations you spoke earlier. Continue until the picture is obliterated completely.

THE DIFFERENT TYPES OF PERSONAL DEMONS

If you're plagued by bad brain habits but can't quite articulate just what is making you feel so down, try envisioning your mental patterns as demons you can fight. Once you know who they are, you can banish them by name. You may want to invent and describe your own, but here are a few we conjured up. Maybe they'll seem familiar.

1. Laab and Lassura: These twins work together to make you feel worthless, no matter what you do. Laab is the demon of apathy, convincing you that no matter how hard you work and how much you try, you will always be worthless and undesirable. Lassura attacks from the other side, telling you that the minute you stop working and ease up on yourself, everyone around you will see you for the fraud you are.

2. Ostriax: This demon is a trickster who can use its powers to alter your perceptions of reality. Its favorite way of playing this game is by persuading you that all your friends are mad at you, don't like you, or are laughing at you behind your back (or all three, if it's feeling playful).

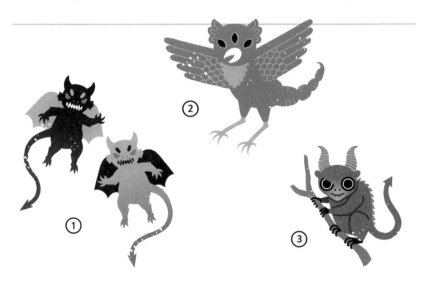

3. Desponon: This demon feeds off of positive energy and self-esteem. Sapped of those qualities, you think of yourself as inherently unworthy of good things and are willing to settle for what is in front of you, because you have no right to expect better.

4. Vindicar: This demon thrives on the misery of others and encourages you to view others' sorrow as your gain. It makes you see success (professional, personal, or emotional) as a ladder, with room for only one at the top, and blocks your access to empathy, forcing you to revel in the failures of others.

5. Avarixas: This demon also enjoys feeling bigger than others but puffs itself up by acquiring new things—luxury goods, grand experiences, even desirable people—not for the pleasure or usefulness of those things, but merely for show. By taking the *best* things, Avarixas believes it is bettered, when all it really does is mask its own insecurity.

6. Culpazion: This demon at once convinces you that you are more powerful than anything and that your power only causes pain and suffering. It convinces you that everything bad that happens is your fault, while anything good is a fluke that has nothing to do with you. Culpazion thrives on false feelings of guilt.

7. Frank: Frank's just a dick. Don't listen to Frank.

A Personal Exorcism Spell

When a personal demon is living in your brain, you need an exorcism. This spell will help you weaken and eventually evict your unwelcome mental guests.

WHAT YOU'LL NEED:

A piece of paper

A black pen and a red pen

Matches

A small, fireproof bowl

Your favorite perfume

When a romantic partner, family member, or boss has treated you badly for a long time, sometimes you internalize their criticism, disapproval, or blame and direct it against yourself even when that person is long gone. It's like they left behind a mean little parasitic demon copy of themselves living in your brain to do their dirty work. Or maybe your internal negative voice isn't a copy of someone, but has been living in your head for as long as you remember, telling you that you're worthless and bad. Either way, an exorcism will take care of it.

On the piece of paper, write in black pen the negative things your inner nemesis tells you about yourself. Be as specific as possible. Maybe you can even write the story of a specific experience that haunts you. Then use the red pen to draw your demon on top of your words. Make it as ugly and vicious as you feel it is.

Fold the paper and place it in the bowl, then light it with a match. As it burns, recite these words:

You hold no power
You are not welcome
I am not what you say I am

Mix the ashes with a few drops of perfume. (If you don't have a favorite perfume, use a bit of olive oil or coconut oil instead.) Dip a finger in the ashes and draw two Xs on yourself, one on your forehead and one on your chest. Recite the incantation again, then shower and wash away the curses. For extra power, mix the remaining ashes into your shampoo, and wash those demons right out of your hair.

WITCH HISTORY
ON DEMONS
AND DAEMONS

FOR HUNDREDS OF YEARS, the word *demon* has connoted a being of pure evil. In texts describing the persecution of accused witches, such as the *Malleus Maleficarum*, demons were consorts of the devil, either controlled by witches to do their evil bidding or sent by the devil to possess them. Sometimes the witches themselves were demons.

However, demons haven't always been evil—and other definitions of the term are much more useful to the modern witch. The word is derived from the ancient Greek δαίμων, or "*daimon*," meaning a guiding spirit. A daimon could be benevolent or evil; essentially it was a powerful force. In Plato's writings, Socrates talks about having a "*daimonion*"—a little daimon—which operated as a kind of spidey-sense, a consciousness that would tell him if what he was about to do was dangerous. According to Plato's *Symposium*, love, too, is a "great daimon" that mediates between humans and gods.

That guiding spirit can be interpreted either as an inner soul or a literal spirit that exists outside the body. Judaism, Hinduism, Zoroastrianism, and many other ancient religions have daimon-like creatures in their mythologies: part-human, part-divine characters that meddle in human affairs, with varying degrees of success. In the Old Testament they were the false idols that the Pagans worshiped and that held no real power.

When the term was imported into the New Testament, it took on the meaning of a malevolent, and real, force. In Acts 16:16–24, the apostles Paul and Silas come upon a slave girl possessed by a demon that allowed her to read fortunes and predict the future. Paul declares: "In the name of Jesus Christ, I command you to leave her!" And the demon leaves, much to the chagrin of the girl's owners, who were profiting from her powers.

In Mark 5, Jesus heals a man possessed by demons who declares, "My name is Legion, for we are many." Jesus drives the demons from him, but the message is clear—demons make you not yourself. They are there only to harm, not to help.

Nowadays, we often spell *daimon* (or *daemon*) and *demon* differently, to distinguish between the two concepts, but they're still easy to confuse (especially if they are spoken aloud rather than written). But the idea of a friendly, if mischievous, spirit that follows you around and tries to help you sounds much more fun than being possessed by an evil monster, and it's an idea that exists in modern culture. Jiminy Cricket, a fairy godmother, and the daemons in *The Golden Compass* are contemporary fictional examples of the guiding spirits we all wish we had.

Listening to your inner voice can take a lot of effort. But thinking of that voice as your guiding daemon, you might find it easier to hear: you're listening not to yourself, but to a trusted confidante who has your best interests at heart. (Or you can listen to an evil demon, but if bad things happen we had nothing to do with it.)

Break Negative Patterns

This spell will help you disrupt damaging repetitive behaviors by facilitating the release of the physical, emotional, or spiritual attachments that hold you back.

WHAT YOU'LL NEED:

A piece of blue string long enough to be tied around your neck

A square of bubble wrap

A bad habit is essentially a commitment—an inadvertent, hurtful commitment of either convenience, fear, or laziness. We procrastinate when we know we should be getting work done. We call the same guy again and again even though he's been passive-aggressive and mean. We keep saying yes to that one friend even though we know we mean no. We commit to doing the same thing over and over, and the pattern becomes harder and harder to break. Change is hard, but not impossible, and symbolically freeing yourself with a spell is a good start.

Loosely tie the blue string, which represents wisdom and clarity, around your neck. Think of the pattern you are trying to break, such as always saying yes to a friend's repeated requests for favors. Imagine a specific example, something you cannot do every single day, like drive them to their soccer practice or spend three hours talking about their relationship. Envision a calendar and, one day at a time, fill the calendar with their requests, until every day is full.

Pick up the bubble wrap, and say:

I release myself from this connection, and I banish it to where it cannot bind me

Pop the bubble wrap one bubble at a time, moving row by row, while repeating the enchantment, until you've popped all the bubbles on the square. Each time you pop a bubble, imagine that day's habit puffing into thin air. When you are done, roll up the bubble wrap, tie the string around it, and throw it in the trash (or recycle it if that's available where you live).

A SPELL TO

Counter Impostor Syndrome

Impostor syndrome is a mind-clouding illusion that makes it impossible for you to see your true potential. This ritual will help you lift the veil from your eyes.

WHAT YOU'LL NEED:

A roll of toilet paper

An index card
or piece of paper

A pen or pencil

The spell is designed to make you feel a little silly while you're doing it. (It involves toilet paper, after all.) Impostor syndrome—the unshakable feeling that, no matter your achievements, you're an undeserving fraud who's going to lose everything once people catch on to your inherent insufficiency—may be a profound and genuine source of anxiety. But if we've learned anything from Harry Potter, it's that the best way to deal with fear is to laugh in its face.

With your eyes closed, wrap the toilet paper around your head so that it covers your eyes. (Wrap it loosely, so that you can open them when you want to.) Continue wrapping until the toilet-paper blindfold is several layers thick. As you wrap, say out loud the things you tell yourself when you're feeling insecure: "You can't do this." "You don't belong here." "Eventually they'll realize you're incompetent."

Once your vision is fully blocked, open your eyes. Imagine a glowing figure becoming dimly visible through the layers of paper. This figure is your best self; concentrate on your achievements, talents, and positive qualities and envision the figure glowing brighter. When the imaginary figure is bright and you feel suffused with warmth and positive energy, rip the blindfold in half and crumple the tissue into a ball.

Examine the crumpled ball, then draw a squiggly line on your paper or index card that represents the shape of the discarded blindfold. Keep this card with you, and trace the line with your finger when you need to wipe your vision clear of undeserved self-doubt.

The Greatest
One-Word Spell: "No"

During the Salem witch trials, judges and witch-hunters were most sus-picious of defiant women: those who refused to answer questions, who called their accusers liars, and who refused to implicate other women. For example, accused witch Sarah Osborne refused to cave to leading questions about her supposed witchy activities. When asked why she hurt children, she said, "I do not hurt them." In transcripts, this appears to infuriate her accuser. In a 1720 essay by Francis Hutchinson, another woman on trial named Sarah Good is quoted as having told interrogators that "I am no more a witch than you are a wizard, and if you take away my life, God will give you blood to drink."

In short, "no" is the word of people who do not obey. It's often said that "no" is a complete sentence, and it's true: those two letters together make one of the most powerful spells that exist. The power of "no" is that it lets you stand up for what you believe in. "No" lets you get what you want. But "no" may also be the hardest sentence in the English language to say.

Although there are many dark and nebulous forces pushing back against your use of it, "no" also contains the ultimate power to defeat them. It can become your Patronus, a bolt of defiant confidence. Here are a few of those forces and how to use your one-word spell to stop them in their tracks.

▶ ▶ ▶ The Blazing Light of Positivity

The implication of the word *no* is, obviously, a negative one. There is a dominant cultural assumption that fulfilling lives are full of yeses and only yeses. (Remember that movie where Jim Carrey discovers how fun life can be once he's forced to say "yes" all the time?) *Yes* is the word of people who are chill, who can go with the flow. Only killjoys say no. Just say yes! But saying no to one thing means saying yes to another. Saying no to a night out could mean saying yes to a much-needed night in, or vice versa.

Of course it's important to push your boundaries and try new things on occasion, but by incorporating no into your vocabulary, you have more control over when and how you choose to let that positive light shine.

▸ ▸ ▸ The Sharp Edge of Rudeness

"No" is also considered a rude response, especially for women, who often are taught to be accommodating and pleasing above all else. If you internalize these beliefs, saying no may seem downright offensive. But think of all the times you've said no and it was perfectly polite. No, you didn't want any more mashed potatoes, even though the presence of mashed potatoes did not deeply offend you. No, you didn't feel like going to the movies that night, but you went the next time. No, you didn't like that book, and nobody was mad. "No" may be definitive and strong, but it doesn't have to be inherently sharp.

▸ ▸ ▸ The Dark Fear of Negativity

Most people are afraid to say "no" because they're worried about the consequences from whomever they're refusing. It's one thing to summon the courage to pass on going on a date or doing a favor, but quite another to deal with the fury and disappointment of the person you turned down. But by using "no" more often, you invoke your power to be in charge of your actions. You are not just agreeing to whatever is presented to you. You're a person with wants and needs, with texture, who knows how to take care of herself in any given moment. Even if you do say "yes" to a chore you don't really want to do, that "yes" is still a choice, rather than something you agree to in order to avoid hurt feelings. Ultimately, saying "no" prioritizes your own feelings over any (real or imagined) reactions from someone else.

Embracing "no" doesn't give you free rein to be a jerk. This spell is as useful for its practical, immediate effects as for its introspective ones. By practicing no, you're paying attention to your own desires, and in turn you can examine whether you've actually meant all the yeses you've said over the years. Maybe by saying no, you'll discover you've actually hated ice skating every time you've gone, or that you like having your weeknights free from not-so-exciting social obligations, or that you'd rather be alone than go on a lackluster date. "Yes" allows you to be giving and nurturing, but the magic of "no" summons your other positive qualities. With it, you can be assertive, protective, or discerning.

Like a lot of spells, invoking "no" can have a profound effect on others. Some may respond with frustration or anger, but in our experience, the spell will turn many friends, partners, and family members into gentler, more understanding people who are better attuned to what you want to say yes to. And that makes your yes even more powerful and special.

OTHER WAYS OF SAYING "NO"

"That won't be possible."

"Can I propose a different idea?"

"That's not really my thing, but you have fun!"

"I just need a night in, you know?"

"I appreciate you asking, but I can't."

"My plate is full right now."
[This may be a white lie, but it's an acceptable one.]

A SPELL FOR

Rejection

Ghosting is reliable only if you're a literal ghost—some people won't take hints, and others deserve a polite but firm dismissal. This spell will help you steel yourself for the difficult goodbye conversation.

WHAT YOU'LL NEED:

A squeezable bottle of honey

Pleasant-smelling liquid soap

Maybe you're on a date, and before dinner is over you can tell you just aren't connecting. But after saying goodnight, you receive a "When can I see you again?" text. Maybe a friend did something to hurt you deeply, but they keep inviting you to coffee despite your repeated excuses. Use this spell to make the "Thanks, but no thanks" conversation easier on you (which will make it easier on them, too).

Grasp the honey in your dominant hand and draw a heart in the open palm of your nondominant hand. Visualize the face of the person you need space from. Say aloud:

I respect your feelings, but I am not responsible for your feelings.

Carefully, without crushing the heart, cover it with soap and turn on the faucet. Rubbing in careful circles, completely wash the honey away.

Backfire!

WHEN SELF-CARE SPELLS GO WRONG

~~~

If you've read any fairy tale or watched any movie about magic, you've seen a wish or spell backfire. Maybe someone wishes that everything he touches turns to gold, then finds he can't pick up a burger without turning it into metal. Maybe someone wishes the goblins would steal her baby brother, but is horrified when they actually do. Magic sometimes works a little *too* well.

Spells for self-care can backfire this way, too. Finally giving yourself permission to put yourself first may feel like a dream come true, but once you start treating yourself more kindly, it's a slippery slope into plain old selfishness. Have cookies for breakfast again? Sure, treat yourself! Skip the birthday party you said you'd go to? Hey, you could use a night in. Demand praise and soothing from your friends? Listen, you deserve it. Self-care seems decadent, but that's just because you're not used to it—right?

Well, maybe, but maybe not. If your self-care magic goes rogue, you become some person who *always* puts herself first, which defeats the purpose of the spell. Lax, permissive self-care—slacking, overindulging, pushing your responsibilities onto others while pampering yourself—may feel good in the moment, but in the long run it saps your energy and seals you off from the people you care about. By that point, it may be too late to stop; self-indulgence can operate like addiction, where you need bigger and bigger hits to feel anything. And the crash gets worse every time.

To avoid going off the rails, tap into personal strength—not just leniency, but self-reliance. Ask yourself a few questions before engaging in self-care, to make sure the spell won't blow up in your face:

✦ What do I gain from this? What does someone else lose? How do those two compare?

✦ Can I differentiate what I want from what I need?

✦ Who am I depending on for help right now? When did I last ask for their support? Do I always seek their help, or do I rely on others, too? Have I offered equivalent support to this person in the past? How long ago?

✦ Will this spell, ritual, or treatment address the symptoms of my troubles or the cause? If it treats only the symptoms, will it make the cause worse?

✦ What is the purpose of relaxing now? Does it let me rest up for future progress, or does it create a block to that progress?

If you notice that any particular self-care spell tends to go awry, try redirecting its energy toward something positive. For instance:

✦ Instead of impulse shopping, buy a gift for a friend, find a homeless shelter's Amazon wish list, purchase something from an organization that donates proceeds to charity, or contribute to a crowdfunding effort. You'll still get the endorphin rush of shopping, but you'll also be giving back.

✦ Instead of sugary comfort food, try hydrating with water, coconut water, or herbal tea. Dehydration sets in quickly when you're distracted, like when you're harried or sad, and makes it harder to cope physically and mentally. Add a little honey for extra sweetness.

✦ Instead of asking for support, offer it. If you're feeling a bit down but aren't dealing with a crisis, you can call your go-to agony aunt, or broadcast your unhappiness on social media, and get enough love to feel better for a day. But remember: reaching out to a friend with words of pride, love, and encouragement makes you feel good *and* strengthens your relationship instead of wearing it down.

Break a Curse

WHAT YOU'LL NEED:

A long white candle

Matches

A bowl

Water

This spell may not stop bad things from happening, but hopefully it will remind you that things won't always be this way.

Many people like to believe that life has some sort of order: actions have reactions, and decisions have consequences. Logic dictates that good and bad things should happen at roughly even intervals.

But that's not how the world works; there is no pattern or constantly balancing scale. The randomness of the universe means that, inevitably, misfortunes will sometimes clump together, with no fun or happy things popping up to compensate. At times like these, you might wonder if you're under a curse.

Clearing away your hopelessness can be the first of many good things to turn your luck around.

Light the candle and let some wax drip into the bottom of the bowl; then use that wax to secure the lit candle upright. The candle should be long enough that the wick extends an inch or two above the bowl's rim.

Fill the bowl with water, and then close your eyes. Imagine the negative events in your life coming together to form a shape of a specific color and size. Maybe it's a tiny red triangle, or a bright yellow rhombus. Hold that shape in your mind long enough for the image to become clear.

Cup your hands in front of you and imagine the shape pouring out of your mind and into your hands, then cascading out of your hands and into the bowl. As this happens, imagine your feelings of inevitability flowing out, too. It's a cliché, but repeat to yourself, "This too shall pass." You'll be surprised how much you need that reminder sometimes.

Once you feel like your negativity has drained, pluck the candle from the bowl and extinguish the flame in the water. Then take the bowl to a sink and wash your hands with the water in the bowl, watching everything that poured into it flowing away.

7

DIVINATION

THE POWER TO DECIDE
YOUR DESTINY

Wouldn't you love magic that works in real life the way it does in *Bewitched*? Wiggle your nose and the person you want to see materializes in your apartment, or your friends forget that embarrassing thing you did, or you suddenly land your dream job.

This is fiction, of course. You can't order around the universe's energy like a butler. The rituals in this book are designed to affect your brain instead of the world, because we can't give you a way to effortlessly manifest your ideal partner, job, wardrobe, or life. Nobody can.

But what about the power to see the future?

Our witchcraft can give you insight about yourself and the world around you—enough insight to foresee what's likely to happen, or at least to figure out what you *want* to happen, the best way to achieve it, and what, if anything, is stopping you.

Gaining such insight may not be easy. Sometimes your ambitions are buried under layers of anxiety or mental blocks. Sometimes you're genuinely uncertain, and no amount of digging into your psyche will reveal one clear, life-changing direction to pursue. But that's all okay. Making peace with the unknown frees you to discover opportunities, choices, and dreams you'd never have considered otherwise.

The trick to finding these things is to speak your desires—or, in a pinch, your uncertainty—out loud, forcing yourself to reckon with it. Many of the rituals we present include an incantation, but sometimes just admitting your hopes and wishes aloud is enough, even without a ritual.

Witchcraft can help you follow your path, but more than that, it can help you create one. Maybe you have a broad idea of what you want out of life and need to narrow it down. Maybe you're choosing between a few options. And maybe the question of life is too big and you feel more comfortable starting small. In this chapter, we'll lay out how to intuit your heart's desire, accept when the crystal ball is dark, and be more comfortable with life's inevitable failures. No matter what, flexing your divination muscles will help you get in touch with your insight. And the stronger it gets, the more unstoppable you become.

Channeling What Lies Beyond

HOW TO CARE FOR YOUR FUTURE SELF

~~~

A recent study by researchers at the University of Zurich found that self-control and empathy depend on the same part of the brain. This makes sense when you think about it: whenever you engage in disciplined behavior, you're doing so out of compassion and kindness to your future self. (Sure, Present You doesn't want to do the dishes before bed, but Morning You *still* won't want to do them, plus she'll be scrambling to get to work. You should cut her a break!) You don't always pay your bills, put things back where they belong, and drag yourself to yoga because these things sound fun. You do them because you have keen empathy for your future self, and you know she'll thank you.

Science may support the connection between self-control and empathy, but it's magic that lets you harness its power. When you're feeling grumpy about chores and other obligations, try summoning a vision of your future self and conversing with her. You can use any ritual you want to summon your future self, but we recommend looking in the mirror in a dim room (maybe a bathroom with the light off but the door open), letting your eyes relax, and saying, "When eye meets eye, may I see I." Then look your reflection in the eye and talk to her as though she's you from tomorrow, next week, or whenever is relevant.

As you're talking, weigh Future You's needs against your current wants: How happy will you be if you put off this obligation? How happy will she be if you do it now? What do you gain, and what does she lose, if you kick the can down the road? What do you lose, and what does she gain, if you just get it over with?

Sometimes, you'll probably still decide to just brush your teeth and go to bed. (Aren't you lucky that you're already standing at the bathroom mirror!) Maybe you're feeling ill, and you'd do a terrible job grocery shopping anyway, and besides, going after work would be more convenient because you'll already be out of the house. But sometimes, the thought of Future You's delight as she slips into crisp clean sheets at the end of the day is more than enough reason to go to the laundromat. All you need to do is ask her and take her answers to heart.

A SPELL TO

Name Your Heart's Desire

This spell uses a variation of a traditional sage burning to trick your secret wish right out of you without you even noticing.

WHAT YOU'LL NEED:

Dried whole sage leaves

A fireproof bowl

A small model or drawing of a heart

Matches

Any number of spells can help make wishes come true, but what if you're having a hard time figuring out what your wish is? You yearn for . . . something, certainly, but your feelings aren't coalescing into tangible thoughts that you can acknowledge, assess, or act on. This spell is like step 0 in that wish-making process, allowing you to tease your desire out of the clouds of uncertainty.

On a table, place the sage in the bowl and prop up the heart behind it. Light the sage and let it smolder, its fragrant smoke filling the air. As you smell it, feel the space around you empty of all concerns and energies.

Looking at the heart, begin talking to yourself out loud about your inner feelings, whatever was concerning you that made you try this spell. You could start with the general topic you believe your inner wish is about, or something as broad as "I feel like I want something, but I don't know what." Say anything that comes into your head. Imagine the words flowing into the heart and then feelings flowing out of it and into you.

If you struggle to find words to say, try to frame your thoughts by completing one of these sentences:

When I picture my future, I see _____ .
When I think of being happy, I am _____ .
What bothers me about my life right now is _____ .
If I could have anything in the world, I'd want _____ .

By speaking thoughts aloud, whatever they are, you'll come closer to revealing your deepest desires.

When the Crystal Ball Is Dark

This ritual will not reveal the future, but it will help you make peace with uncertainty and trust that whatever decisions you make will bring you value and knowledge.

WHAT YOU'LL NEED:

A white candle

Matches

A coin

If you're at a crossroads in your life and unsure of your next step, there's no way you can force yourself into knowing what you want. In a society where everyone is encouraged to be ambitious and have a plan (or at least know what they want to be for the rest of their lives when they're 17), letting yourself live in the unknown can be incredibly anxiety inducing. This practice will help keep you calm in the presence of uncertainty.

Light the candle and place it in front of you on a flat surface. Spin the coin in front of the candle and let it fall where it may. Pick it up and keep spinning it, as you recite the following:

Heads or tails I do not know
But it matters not
The coin is still a coin
Whichever face it shows

Heads or tails I do not know
But it matters not
My life is still my own
Whichever path I travel

Recite this incantation as many times as you need until you feel comforted. Sleep with the coin under your pillow for one night.

The Alchemy of Failure

HOW TO CREATE
GOLDEN OPPORTUNITIES

~~~

Many of us are held back from flying bravely into the future, not because we don't want to take charge and soar but simply because we're burdened with anxiety. Sometimes we worry about big, uncontrollable things. (What if I get sick, or if someone in my family does? What if the economy tanks? What if there's a huge earthquake and my state falls into the ocean?) But the rest of the time, probably most of the time, that anxiety boils down to a fear of failure.

Fear of failure doesn't just keep you from leaping into the future. It also keeps you from all the steps on the path: planning, stating your goals, and creating changes. Fear of failure keeps your head down and stops you from looking beyond what you already have. It keeps you from doing the basic, liberating magic of naming your heart's desire.

Worry is healthy when it protects you from making the kinds of flying leaps that can cause physical harm, catastrophic debt, or mental health disaster. But worrying about things like rejection, looking stupid, disappointing parents or peers—these fears rarely deserve the weight we invest in them. The good news is, they tend to crumble when you realize that no evaluation of your performance in life is more important than your own. What does failure even mean for women who are joyfully unruly and happy to live outside society's expectations? Sure, we know that the masses have long been happy to judge and punish these women for imagined crimes, outlandish acts, and things done wrong, improperly, or not at all. But these days, nobody's going to burn you at the stake for a screw-up, real or imagined. If someone judges your romantic choices, your workplace challenges, your creative efforts, your style of dress, who cares? They can put you on trial, but you don't have to show up to court.

The first step in defeating failure is embracing your unruliness and recognizing that operating outside the norm is *kind of your thing*. You don't have to accept the lead weight of your fear as an immovable burden. You can refashion it into something more precious and helpful. By using your fear of failure (or even actual failure) as an ingredient in a bigger magical work, you can apply a little alchemy and transmute your setback into success. Here are a few ways to make it happen.

INGREDIENT ▸ Dropping the ball on an obligation, task, or deadline

Use for ▸ A centering spell. Consider the situation that led you to forget your responsibility. Did you have too much on your plate? Do you lack a good way of keeping track of tasks? Was the thing you were asked to do beyond your abilities in some way, and do you need to learn to delegate? See this failure as a way to evaluate your organizational and support systems, and seek out more help or structure where needed.

INGREDIENT ▸ Failing to get something—a job, a grant, entry to an educational program—you worked hard for

Use for ▸ A scrying spell. Identifying what exactly about this opportunity appealed to you can refine your vision for the future or isolate a specific, single wish you can fulfill in other ways. (Once when Jess was turned down for a job, she realized that she was upset less about the gig and more because it was close to home, which would have enabled her to get a dog. So she just got a dog.)

INGREDIENT ▸ Trying to learn a new skill and kind of sucking at it

Use for ▸ A mind-melding spell. Seek out examples of others who have enthusiastically messed something up: videos of cats trying to jump onto things and missing, collections of Pinterest fails, music that's bad on purpose (try the Portsmouth Sinfonia or Smith College's Crapapella a cappella group, which is the ne plus ultra of gleeful failure), or the YouTube videos of Simone Giertz, a robotics enthusiast whose creations just flail and flop around. Once you've observed one of these particularly joyful failures, try to sink into that same feeling. What if, instead of beating yourself up for not immediately performing to a high standard, you were just enjoying the hell out of this new activity?

INGREDIENT ▸ Embarrassing yourself in public

Use for ▸ A strengthening spell. More often than not, the horror of making a fool of yourself is way worse in the abstract; once it happens, you realize you can handle it. Check in with yourself: do you still have all your best qualities? Check in with your friends: do they still like you? Chances are, all is well. You faced embarrassment and came through with your self-concept and relationships intact. You tested your mettle and survived. Hang on to the knowledge of this strength for next time.

HOW TO READ TEA LEAVES

Tasseography is the time-honored art of reading tea leaves (or coffee grounds) to see the future. Many cultures believe that, by brewing and drinking a cup of loose-leaf tea, swirling the dregs, and turning the cup upside down, the leaves will form a specific shape that you can interpret to see what lies ahead. There are tons of possible interpretations, but here are a few to get you started.

Star
Good luck and fortune await.

Heart
You will find love or friendship.

Sword
You will have an argument.

Door or arch
A new opportunity will arise.

Flower
You will receive praise.

Owl
Things are not what they seem.

Leonardo's *Last Supper*
Your cup is too big.

Cow
You will see a cow.

Clump of tea leaves
You've just had some tea.

UR GONNA DIE
This one could mean anything.

Embracing Failure

WHAT YOU'LL NEED:

A blindfold

A pen

A piece of paper

Colored pencils, crayons, or other art supplies

This spell lets you practice being confused and clumsy and still fall in love with whatever happens.

When you try something unfamiliar, it stands to reason that you won't do a perfect job. You're unclear exactly how it works, you haven't practiced, and you don't know the tricks or the rules. But sometimes you're better off doing something imperfectly than doing it by the book—and doing it imperfectly is always better than not doing it at all. Practicing imperfection will allow you to be more flexible when and if failure does arrive.

Cover your eyes with the blindfold (or just close them). Hold the pen in your dominant hand and the paper in your other hand. Raise your hands and say aloud: "I welcome darkness. I welcome confusion. I welcome failure and the gifts it brings."

Spin around seven times widdershins (counterclockwise). Sit on the floor and, while you're still dizzy, immediately draw three pictures: yourself, an animal to represent the natural world (you can use the animal you chose for "Which Pet Should Be Your Familiar?" on page 96), and a celestial object to represent the spiritual world.

When you're finished drawing, remove the blindfold and look at your masterpiece. You'll likely discover a bunch of squiggly lines that barely resemble what you were trying to draw. Turn the paper 90 degrees. Contemplate the drawing from this perspective, and identify the parts you like best—maybe they look like what you meant to draw, maybe they look like something else entirely, or maybe they're just beautifully abstract. With the crayons or colored pencils, decorate these parts of the drawing, turning them into small works of art. When you are finished, hold the paper to your heart and say aloud, "My failure is beautiful. My failure is something new."

Hang the finished work on your fridge for a week, or display it near your desk or workspace. If fear of failure has been holding you back from a specific project or pursuit, keep the drawing up until you make a good-faith effort at starting. Then tear the picture into tiny pieces and release it into the wind.

WITCH HISTORY

THE MYTH OF
MOTHER SHIPTON

THE RENAISSANCE-ERA ENGLISH SOOTHSAYER Ursula "Mother" Shipton was in many ways the epitome of the witch. She had mysterious origins, a quarrelsome temperament, and an intuitive nature. She is known now for being the "Northern Prophetess," an oracle that predicted the future, and her "cave" is now a tourist attraction in England. But overall, she just seems like a smart woman.

As the most popular origin myth goes, Shipton, born in 1488, had no father but was sired by the Phantom of Apollo, just like Merlin before her. (Other theories claim her father was a necromancer.) Although the Merlin-esque origin story is certainly flattering, more likely the truth is that Shipton (and Merlin, maybe) was simply born out of wedlock, and the people of her town invented supernatural explanations to understand the seeming total impossibility of an unmarried woman getting pregnant.

Necromancer dad or no, Shipton's birth scandalized the neighbors and they accused her mother, Agatha, of being a witch. Agatha reportedly was brought to court, but before the judge could punish her for "Incontinency," she pointed out that he himself had impregnated two women outside of marriage, so it'd be pretty hypocritical for him to judge her. Clearly, these women came from a long line of badasses.

As an adult, Shipton apparently had the appearance of a classic evil witch: long nose, pimples, and hunched posture, at least according to a 1667 description by Richard Head (granted, this was written more than a hundred years later and at the height of the prosecution of witches to boot). Supposedly, she married a Toby Shipton when she was 24, though he died a few years later, and she spent most of her life around her cave near Knaresborough, Yorkshire. There, she gathered plants and herbs and brew them into potions, despite taunting by the nearby townspeople (many of whom secretly sought out her brews anyway). In temperament, she was less demonically driven than cheerfully vindictive: she played "merry pranks" on those who abused her, according to 1775's *The Wonderful History and Surprising Prophecies of Mother Shipton*. When some guy dared to call her the "devil's bastard" and "hag face," she reportedly used magic to steal his hat off his head and replace it with a portable toilet.

Shipton is best known for being a soothsayer. She predicted the futures of those around her and of the world at large, seemingly to anyone who would listen. She is credited with predictions about everything from train travel to the telegraph to the dissolution of the Catholic Church. Though she was a contemporary of Nostradamus, she never attained the fame of the renowned (male) seer—give you one guess why—but her visions were recorded by others.

Except those visions were all made up. Her "prophecies" were published centuries after her death, and some authors even admitted that they faked them and attributed them all to her. So why choose to credit this woman? Perhaps the soothsayer myth was based somewhat in truth—with the written accounts made so long after her death, we'll never know what she did or didn't say. Or perhaps Mother Shipton had a reputation for being particularly intuitive. Women have long been relegated to the role of observer, rather than actor, and when all your energy is put into observation, you can't help but notice things. An "ugly" woman born out of wedlock would certainly have been on the sidelines of early modern English society (plus, there was the whole living-in-a-cave thing), so Shipton probably had a lot of time to think, take notice, and, perhaps, become an insightful student of human nature.

Whatever Mother Shipton was like when alive, her myth has only grown stronger as the years pass. Today, she is hailed as a mystic, a prophet, and a sorceress. But she was also a woman who lived a hard life and who maybe understood just a little bit more about other human beings than they were able to perceive themselves. Often, that's all a witch is and all we need to claim the title ourselves. May we all get the cool cave monuments we deserve.

Navigating Flawed Visions

WHAT TO DO WHEN
PREDICTIONS GO AWRY

～～～

You may not have visions of the future like Phoebe from *Charmed*, but we all have some amount of power to predict what will happen. Sometimes you can tap into those abilities using a crystal ball, a tarot deck, or other tools that help you listen. But you also put your precognitive abilities to work, without really thinking about it, every time you make a plan.

Unfortunately, your natural power to predict the future sometimes goes wrong.

Sometimes, you invest in the idea of a positive future that ultimately does not come to pass. You plan for it, you picture it in detail, you count on it, and then it falls through. You're now living in a present you never thought could happen, and maybe you've lost the ability to trust yourself.

Witches are nothing if not resilient, but when you're shocked into a future you never envisioned, conjuring your strength and resolve can seem impossible. And platitudes like "stay strong" or "don't worry" offer little help, because if you knew how to stay strong, presumably you'd be doing it already. How can you tap into your strengths at a moment when you feel bewildered and weak?

▶ ▶ ▶ **Assess what went wrong.**
When the future is unfolding in ways you didn't expect, return to your tools to figure out what happened. Mastery of clairvoyance requires unbiased assessment of the information you're receiving, which for most people is incredibly difficult. A little retrospective examination can help hone your intuition. Ask yourself: Were you pushing your interpretation toward what you *wanted* to happen? Were you ignoring red flags that pointed to reality? Was there an inside voice that you had a hard time listening to?

▶ ▶ ▶ Keep your eyes forward.

Don't let self-assessment keep you bogged down in past mistakes. Remember: magic is made of small acts that build into lasting change. The past may be done, but the future is not fixed. In times of crisis, return to small things that make you feel capable and competent to help you focus. Then use that focus to take action toward determining the future you want.

▶ ▶ ▶ Tap into your power.

What makes you feel powerful? Lighting some incense and meditating? Convening with your coven to make plans for action? Cooking for others to make your community feel safe and loved? Whatever it is, now's the time to do it. It may not feel like much in the face of your scary new future, and it won't immediately transform things into a happier circumstance. But hopefully it *will* help you reclaim your power in a time of helplessness and show the world that you still have some control.

An opposite scenario can happen, too: you're so convinced that a future plan will result in disaster that you never start trying to make it, which means that you never get a chance to be proven wrong. When you're paralyzed by dark visions, magic can help you snap out of your funk and build a more realistic idea of the future.

▶ ▶ ▶ Enchant your mind with an amulet.

Sometimes you're bogged down by fears you can't shake because your brain just can't figure out how to stop obsessing (even if it wants to). Give it an excuse to calm down by using a magical amulet of strength and protection. This could be a piece of jewelry or a watch or pin you wear every day, but the amulet may be more effective if you hunt for a new one that feels just right. (For more, see page 44.) Every time you wear it or notice its weight around your neck or finger, let its presence draw your mind out of the nebulousness of the future and back into the certainty of the present.

▶ ▶ ▶ Focus on what you can change.

It's easy to feel defeated by big worries on the horizon, but you'll be better equipped to cope with the winds of fate if you have control over your broom. Think small: what can you do to make the future more approach-able? You don't have to solve everything right now, but you can help bolster yourself by attacking small, manageable problems. Even a task as insignificant as opening a document or addressing an envelope can banish a bit of fear.

▸ ▸ ▸ Tell a tale.

Witches are creatures of folklore, so if you're stuck on one dire vision of the future, try tapping into the profound power of storytelling. Spin a yarn about the worst thing that could happen, then one about the best possible outcome, and finally a bunch of stories about various options in between. What might you do in each situation, and how does that change the ending? If the worst truly came to pass, what concrete steps could you take to improve the situation? Envisioning specifics will help you feel more prepared and calm you down.

Keep Going

Like many traditional spells for seeing the future, this modified scrying spell uses a reflective surface as a medium. You can use any small, handheld object that reflects light— even the screen of your cell phone.

WHAT YOU'LL NEED:

A small, handheld reflective surface, such as a mirror or a cell phone

Traditional witches and sorcerers might tell the future, or scry, by peering into a body of water, a bowl of ink, or—you guessed it—a crystal ball, but you can use anything you have on hand.

We all have times when the future seems overwhelmingly difficult, meaningless, or fraught with peril. These are times to call on your coven, to care for yourself and the people you love. But they're also times when magic can remind you that all is never lost. (Some, maybe! Lots, even! But not all.)

Even when you can't choose your future, you can choose how you react to it: Dread or anticipation? Galvanization or despair? When fear and anxiety keep you from clearly seeing what needs to be done and what's on the horizon, this spell will help you focus.

While standing, stare at your reflection in the reflective surface and let your eyes relax until your vision blurs. Say aloud:

The future is dark
The future holds fright
Show me my solid ground
Show me my light

Continue looking at your reflection and relaxing your eyes, imagining that you are looking at a dense cloud or fog bank. This is your anxiety and despair, clouding your vision.

Think of one single, simple concrete action you can take to help things go right (or at least less wrong). It should be simple: instead of "apply for jobs," think "send one cover letter"; instead of "pack up the apartment," think "put my dishes in a box." Look down, moving your scrying surface with your gaze so that it stays in front of your eyes. Picture a cairn of rocks jutting up through the fog. This is your simple concrete action, your solid ground.

Next, think of one thing, however small, that you're looking forward to. It can be soon or far off, big or small: a vacation, a movie with a friend, this Sunday's crossword puzzle, your afternoon snack. Look up, moving the scrying surface with your gaze so that it stays in front of your eyes. Picture a star burning through the fog. This is your light, your reminder that the future holds at least one promise.

Close your eyes and stand for a moment with your feet solidly planted, feeling warmed by the light. The spell is done, but you can repeat it anytime you feel overwhelmed.

DIY Rituals

HOW TO MAKE YOUR OWN SPELL

〰

As we've mentioned, predicting the future is an imprecise art. You can't anticipate everything, and even with lots of precaution and probing of what's to come, there will always be outcomes you didn't plan for. For this reason, no one book could ever contain every spell you'll ever need.

Luckily, our kind of witchcraft is adaptable. You can use this book as a starting point for creating spells tailor-made for your individual goals and challenges. After all, the spells in this book don't summon any supernatural powers to do your bidding. They don't need the approval of a magical counsel. They're effective because they help you focus, think, breathe, and act, using ritual and fire and some words that you might feel silly saying out loud. A spell you make yourself will work just as well—and in some cases, better—to give you clarity.

Building a spell requires deep thought about symbolism, meaning, and what objects and words inspire power in you. Here are some ways you can go about constructing one for yourself.

① Think about the tone of your spell.

Figure out how you want your spell to make you feel, and think about what textures or colors create that feeling—this will help determine not just the setting and style of your spell, but the materials used. Is the spell's desired effect fueled by passion, heat, and fire or peacefulness, coolness, and water? For a spell about love, for example, you might use a red candle instead of a blue one to symbolize passion. For a spell about making amends, you'll want to use something made of a soft and giving material to evoke flexibility and comfort.

② Consider your objects.

Aside from colored candles or herbs and oils that represent different energies, choose spell objects that have personal resonance with the things you're trying to accomplish. Having an emotional tie to a spell always increases its strength. Does the smell of toasting marshmallows soothe you? Devise a centering ritual around roasting them. Does your grandmother's wool blanket make you feel safe? Use it in a protection spell. If the spell relates to another person, incorporate an item of their clothing or a photo of the person to enhance your perception of them.

③ Mark your words.

An incantation can make your practice feel more grounded and active than a spell that involves only actions or thoughts. In fact, finding the right words can be part of the magic: as you literally articulate your desires, you mentally home in on the specifics of what you want. Your incantation can use the name of the person you're trying to influence (even if it's you), call on gods or powers you want to help you, or just plainly state the thing you want again and again. It doesn't even have to rhyme!

④ Create a beginning, middle, and end.

Think of a spell as a workout. Start with a warm-up: setting up your tools (lighting candles, pouring water, arranging things) and taking a moment to set your intentions and feel comfortable in your space. Next comes the heavy lifting, the main event, where you perform the ritual you've designed to attract the desired outcome (cooking something, binding a doll, drawing a magic rune) or speak the words of an incantation. Finally, the cool-down slowly draws you out of the spell, which can be as easy as thanking yourself for making the effort.

⑤ Mean it.

A spell doesn't have to be a major production with incense and crystals and a hundred steps. It can be, if that's what makes it feel real to you, but it can also be a quiet moment you take for yourself with no accessories or poetry. What matters is whether you believe it. Sometimes the ritual is a way to spark a belief or emotion that isn't yet present inside you. Other times it's simply a way to organize what you already feel. But no matter what your goal or method, some part of you should be comforted, delighted, or moved by the process. You should feel like you're making magic.

HOW TO HARNESS THE ELEMENTS

Fire: Fire represents energy, love, passion, and power, which can quickly turn to anger. It is represented in spells by burning candles, lighting incense, or incorporating ashes, and its associative colors are red, orange, and gold (you know, fire colors). If you're kitchen witching, channel fire through chili, cinnamon, or garlic.

Water: Water is the element of emotions, and it is also used for purification and seeking wisdom. You can utilize it in spells by drinking it, submerging other objects in it, or washing yourself in it. It can be useful in spells designed to get you in touch with feminine qualities.

Earth: Earth is a *grounding* element (get it?) that represents stability and calm as well as abundance, strength, and growth. Using stones, dirt, wood, or herbs in spells are all ways to incorporate earth, as well as earthy colors like green and brown. Crystals are also a good choice to incorporate in earth-based spells.

Air: Air is the element of the mind and of freedom. It is used in spells for intelligence, psychic powers, or any kind of release and relaxation. Because air is more difficult to harness than earth or water, many witches invoke its power with a wand. Air can also work in tandem with fire through the act of blowing out incense or candles. Its associated season is spring, the time of new beginnings and new life.

New Endeavors

WHAT YOU'LL NEED:

A small yellow candle

A butter knife

Matches

A phone or other music player

A cushion or comfortable chair

If something is tough to start or will be tough to continue, or both, it's worth taking a moment—and perhaps casting a spell—to mark your new endeavor.

As a culture, we already have a lot of rituals to mark the launch of something momentous and new: exchanging rings, moving the tassel on your mortarboard, breaking a bottle of champagne over the prow of a ship. But what about smaller, personal efforts? Sometimes we might need a ritual—like this one—for putting in a load of laundry, starting that work project, or even getting out of bed in the morning.

Queue up three songs on your phone or music player: one soothing song, one midtempo song, and one energizing song (make sure you'll be able to skip easily from one to the next). You'll want to use a smaller candle—like a birthday or Chanukah candle—for this ritual, since a votive candle burns too slowly. Using the butter knife (or a toothpick), make three marks on the candle: one a quarter inch to a half inch down from the top, one a quarter inch to a half inch down from that, and the third another quarter inch to half inch down from that.

Start playing the soothing song, and sit in a comfortable place with the candle in front of you. Light the candle and say aloud, "Ready."

Watch the candle burn and think about the history of your new endeavor. How did you get to this point? How have you prepared yourself?

When the candle burns down to your first mark, stand up (or move in a way that uses an increasing level of energy), change to the midtempo song, and say aloud, "Set."

Remain standing and keep watching the candle. Envision the first steps of your new endeavor. How will you begin?

When the candle burns down to your second mark, change to the energizing song, and say aloud, "go." Start moving. You can decide how much effort you want to use—whether this is dancing or running in place or just wiggling your arms. Picture yourself succeeding in your new endeavor. What will success look like? What are your goals?

When the candle burns to your third mark, blow it out. You're ready. Go.

ACKNOWLEDGMENTS

We would like to extend our warmest thanks to editorial sorceress Blair Thornburgh for her textual wizardry; to our agent Kate McKean for representing us and for having the idea in the first place; to our amazing illustrator Camille Chew for making us want to be every woman she drew in the book; to designers Andie Reid and Molly Murphy for bringing all of this to life (but not in a necromancy way); to Nicole De Jackmo and the publicity team at Quirk for their commitment; to our partners, Matt and Justin, for unconditional support and cute butts; to the Snails for being our coven of cheerleaders; to the lovely Hannah Giorgis for her help about hair; to Enchantments on E. 9th for the candles we burned in our "we're gonna write a book" ritual which totally worked because magic is real; and to our familiars: Huxley, Dot, and Ophelia (who is very important).

ABOUT THE AUTHORS

~~~

Jaya Saxena is a staff writer at Elle.com. Her work has appeared in many outlets including the *New Yorker*, the *Daily Dot*, the *Toast*, *BuzzFeed*, *Eater*, and many others.

Jess Zimmerman is a contributing editor at the *Establishment*. Her writing has been published in the *Guardian*, the *New Republic, Atlas Obscura, Hazlitt*, the *Hairpin*, the *Toast, Eater, Aeon*, and others.

ABOUT THE ILLUSTRATOR

~~~

Camille Chew is an illustrator whose work explores themes of mythology, fantasy, and the occult. She is a graduate of Alfred University and is based in Ithaca, New York.